LEGENDS
of
DEVON

Sally Jones

BOSSINEY BO(

GW00645227

First published in 1981
by Bossiney Books
St Teath, Bodmin, Cornwall
Designed, typeset and printed in Great Britain by
Penwell Ltd., Parkwood, Callington
Cornwall

ISBN 0 906456 52 5

PLATE ACKNOWLEDGMENTS

Cover by Ray Bishop
Drawings by Paul Honeywill
Pages 7, 17, 27, 29, 30, 69, 70, 82, 91 Roy J. Westlake
Pages 9, 22, 44-47, 54-57, 60, 68, 73, 74, 76, 78 Ray Bishop
Pages 18, 24, 94, 98 Alice Lennox-Boyd
Pages 83, 86 Sharp's Studio
Page 37 Western Morning News
Page 38 Jim Thorington
Page 11 David C. Golby
Page 63 Chris Chapman
Page 75 Joan Rendell

ABOUT THE AUTHOR

Devon is a mine of folklore and myth — so much so that some of the legends have become part of the Devon landscape. Myth, over the years, has been the inspiration of great story-telling. Here in a journey through legendary Devon, Sally Jones brings into focus some fascinating tales, making us wonder whether there can be any such thing as total myth without a shred of reality. She shows us that the line dividing fact and legend is an intriguing one — like Dartmoor on a misty morning. Beautiful drawings and photographs complete this journey among the legendary sites of this lovely county.

Sally Jones was educated at King Edward VI High School for Girls, Birmingham, and read English at St Hugh's College, Oxford, where she won five Blues — tennis, squash, modern pentathlon, netball and cricket. She was British Schoolgirl tennis champion and has played squash for Devon and tennis and squash for Warwickshire. In 1976 she won the *Sunday Telegraph* writing prize of £500 for an account of a tour of Ireland with the British Universities tennis team. More recently she won a prize in the Catherine Pakenham Memorial Awards for Young Women Journalists. In 1978 she joined the BBC as a News Trainee and the following year she moved to Westward TV as a television reporter on Westward Diary.

In 1980 Bossiney published her first book *Legends of Cornwall*, an immediate best-seller. This is its natural successor.

3

LEGENDS of DEVON

Are legends idle fancy or the high-water mark of history, the residue of ancestral memories left after the tide of events has receded?

Certainly history has played a part in the making of many of Devon's legends. Sir Francis Drake figured prominently, not just as the sea-discoverer and conquerer of the Spaniards, but as a supernaturally powerful benefactor. In one tale, he bewitches a Dartmoor stream and leads it into town at the heels of his horse to provide the people of Plymouth with a water-supply. In another, he becomes a Ulysses figure who returns from his long wanderings in disguise to test his wife's fidelity. Before this, he loosed off a cannonball through the centre of the earth which burst forth at the altar between his fiancée and the man she was poised to marry, thinking Drake was dead.

The facts are more prosaic. At a time when water was scarce and supplies chancy, Drake obtained an Act of Parliament to build artificial channels from Dartmoor across private land into a reservoir north of Plymouth. The stream arrived to an accompaniment of public merry-making. The corporation in full dress and chains of office came out to meet it amid much firing of cannon, one root perhaps of the cannonball story.

This sort of basis in reality is common to most of the legends. It is the way in which the popular imagination has welded fantasy to truth to transform events like the opening of the Plymouth leat into glittering myth. Browning describes a similar creative process by comparing it to the making of a Tuscan ring which is fashioned from a mixture of pure gold and alloy.

When the shape of the ring has been made, the craftsman directs

Sir Francis Drake bewitches a Dartmoor stream. ▶

a spurt of acid onto the surface; the alloy is dissolved and the fine filigree of pure gold remains. Correspondingly, in the creative process, the gold — or truth — is mixed with the alloy of fancy to produce the filigree work of legend:

> Now, as the ingot, ere the ring was forged,
> Lay gold (beseech you hold that figure fast)
> So . . . lay absolutely truth, fanciless fact . . .
> . . . Thence bit by bit I dug
> The lingot truth that memorable day,
> Assayed and knew my piecemeal gain was gold.
>
> Yes, but from something else surpassing that,
> Something of mine which mixed up with the gold
> Made it bear hammer and be firm to file.
> Fancy with fact is just one fact the more
> To whit, that fancy has infused, transpierced.
> I fused my live soul and that inert stuff
> Before attempting smithcraft.

It is the live soul of the Devon people, superstitious, hero-worshipping, imaginative, that informs the legends, making them more than half-remembered history or the remnants of folk-memory.

With such a rich store to choose from, I have at times selected those which despite a historical basis, have become legends through exaggeration and imaginative additions to documented events. The unremittingly rascally life of Bampfylde Carew, king of the beggars, is an indulgence I permitted myself on these grounds, for it is taken from his autobiography which rivals Baron Munchausen's in its exuberant inventiveness.

The squeamish may flinch at my choice of so many blood-thirsty and horrific tales but, like folk-songs, many of the best legends possess a black twist. I must admit too, that my own taste runs to the macabre, particularly Faustian pacts with the Devil, in which the pact-maker is satisfyingly carried off to hell in a blaze of sparks, oaths and sulphur fumes. In some cases, the wrong-doers are still visible in the form of rocks. The Parson and the Clerk near Teignmouth and Ragged Dick and his friends in the Valley of Rocks at

In the Valley of Rocks at Lynton. ▶

6

Lynton are just two of the more spectacular sites and, as in Cornwall, many of the stone circles are believed to be maidens turned to stone for dancing on the Sabbath.

So the legends have become part of the Devon landscape, but the greatest can stand apart, both from the events that engendered them and the stones that preserve their memory, holding their own as magical examples of the story-teller's art, as durable and timeless as the Dartmoor tors.

BRUTUS AND CORINEUS

There is nothing modest about the legends of Devon. The county claims to be the site of the founding of Britain, no less, and points to a worn, granite boulder in Totnes as proof. The story starts with the sack of Troy when the great hero Brutus, grandson of Aeneas, struggled beneath the yoke of the Greek overlords. He gathered a group of loyal, dispossessed Trojans about him and sailed away to rid his nostrils of the stench of blood and death and burning rubble. Weeks later, they arrived at a desert island and found a ruined temple among the trees. The shattered columns and fallen shrine symbolised to them their beloved Troy and they lit three fires in honour of their gods. A silvery flash showed between the trees and they glimpsed a rare white hart, a prize indeed. Silently, they stalked it through the undergrowth and at length caught it beside the altar where they sacrificed it and mixed its blood with wine in a great goblet. Each drank deeply then lay down to sleep, Brutus wrapped in the skin of the hart.

At the turn of the night he awoke to unearthly music and saw a radiantly beautiful woman gliding towards him, the new moon in her hair and a sceptre in her hand, the morning star shining at its point. When she spoke, her words chimed like a carillon of silver bells and her luminous green eyes looked beyond Brutus into the past and the future:

'You will sail far, far away to find a fertile island. Here you will rule in triumph and found a great race of heroes who will bear your

The Author at Hound Tor. ▶

name valiantly forever.'

The beautiful woman vanished, leaving only a faintly golden haze and Brutus at once roused his comrades. They, too, were fired by the magnificent vision and at dawn they set sail. After weeks of heaving seas and gales, they reached a spectacular estuary and each knew in his heart they were on the right track. They sailed up the great river on the flood tide, along the lush, steep-sided valley. Then at a tiny hamlet, they beached the boats. Brutus was the first to step ashore, and, if generations of Devon schoolboys are to be believed, declaimed:

> *Here I sit and here I rest*
> *And this spot shall be called Totnes.*

It seems a strange choice of words since the English language did not evolve for centuries, though perhaps it was a later, colloquial translation of his own tongue. Certainly the Brutus stone, where he first set foot in what was then called Albion, is preserved in the wall of 37, High Street in Totnes. The granite slab has been worn smooth by water and bears an imprint like a footstep. That is why I prefer the story of Brutus to the other explanation of the stone: Brutus, say the sceptics, is merely a corruption of the French word *bruitier*, or town-crier, so the *bruitier's* or Brutus stone was the place where he would broadcast the latest news to the people of Totnes. For me, belief in the arrival of Brutus and his Trojans is as alluring as the idea of the boy Christ coming to Cornwall with Joseph of Arimathea. It certainly has an equally distinguished pedigree, as both Geoffrey of Monmouth and Milton refer to it off-handedly as if it were accepted historical fact.

Like most conquerors, Brutus rewarded his loyal captains handsomely. Each was given a region of the newly-christened Britain to rule and Corineus, Brutus' most trusted friend, was given first choice. Predictably, he chose the most beautiful part of all, the West-country. This was not purely on aesthetic grounds. Corineus was a hunting man, and after the most dangerous big game of all — giants. When Brutus arrived, they were plentiful throughout the land, but

The Brutus Stone at Totnes 'bears an imprint like a footstep.' ▶

he slaughtered many and drove the shambling survivors of the monstrous race into the mountain fastness of the West, to the honeycomb caves along the South Devon coast and into the Cornish cairns and high moors.

Corineus loved wrestling above everything else and as Brutus' champion he had killed many of the giants in single combat. The giants banded together and brooded on revenge. They drank deep draughts of mead from bejewelled goblets in their caverns underground and always the toast was:

'Death to Brutus who has robbed us of our land, and destruction to Corineus who has slain so many of our comrades.'

Their leader was a towering hulk, twelve cubits high, called Gogmagog. He was so strong, he could uproot a fully-grown oak, strip off the branches as if they were celery leaves and wield the massive trunk like a hazel wand.

Brutus held the high festival of Thanksgiving to the Gods at Totnes on the anniversary of his landing there, but unknown to the Britons in the neighbouring hills the giants lay in wait. In the midst of the solemn ceremonies, the sacrifices and the feasting, in burst Gogmagog, roaring, raging and whacking to left and right with his deadly club. The other giants followed where he led, ripping off the Trojans' limbs with their teeth which were filed into points and wrenching heads from bodies. One snatched up the sacred sacrificial knife and cut out the heart of everyone within reach. Another ripped out his victim's entrails and smeared them across the high altar in a ghoulish parody of Brutus' sacrifice of a goat. The slaughter was unimaginable as the Britons were unprepared and defenceless. It was no time to make a stand and Brutus and Corineus with a bare handful of the other lords slashed their way to the door and escaped. They then gathered at Plymouth for the great show-down. The giants for once refrained from their goblets of mead and drunken orgies for they realised just how fierce the battle would be.

At the first onslaught, half the giants fell, too slow-moving and slow-witted to escape the thrusts of the British swords. Brutus' men also suffered heavy losses but the speediest stayed out of range of the gigantic hands. Soon only the ferocious Gogmagog was left alive and Corineus begged leave of Brutus to be allowed to take him

◀ Corineus confronts the giant Gogmagog in single combat.

13

on in single-combat. Brutus assented and Corineus, dressed only in a tunic, stepped out on Plymouth Hoe to confront the giant. Gogmagog growled into his beard, then curling his upper lip to reveal his pointed fangs in a great snarl, he crushed Corineus in his arms and lifted him above his head. His grasp crushed three of the Trojan's ribs and the bulging muscles tightened slowly to finish him off. Suddenly, Corineus was transformed by rage and with a mighty wrench he tore himself from the giant's clutches, then heaved him into the air on his shoulders. Staggering under the massive weight, he ran to the nearest shore and hurled him down onto the sharp-fanged rocks below. Gogmagog's blood flowed out to sea, dyeing the whole expanse of Plymouth Sound crimson for as far as the eye could see.

Tales of Gogmagog survive in numerous versions. Two great effigies have stood at the Guildhall in London for centuries. The present figures replaced a pair destroyed in the blitz, while these in their turn dated from the Great Fire of London which consumed their predecessors. Although they are now called Gog and Magog, Queen Elizabeth I knew them as Corineus and Gogmagog.

In the eleventh century, Geoffrey of Monmouth mentioned Lam Goëmagot or Gogmagog's leap and this has perhaps surfaced in the name Lamhay Hill which leads from Sutton to the Citadel. Later, two giants were cut into the hillside to mark the site of the epic struggle. As there is no chalk there and the Hoe is solid limestone, the figures were picked out with red earth from nearby. Accounts survive of the cleaning and reddening of at least one figure in Tudor times. The Plymouth Corporation audit book records:

1529 - 30   Cleansing of Gog Magog 8d.
1566 - 7   20d. New cutting the Gogmagog.

By 1602, a second figure, probably of Corineus had been added as Richard Carew observed in his *Survey of Cornwall*:

'Moreover upon the Hawe at Plymouth there is cut in the ground the portrayture of two men, the one bigger, the one lesser, with clubbes in their hands (whom they term Gogmagog) and (as I have learnt) it is renewed by order of the Townsmen when cause requireth, which should infer the same to be a monument of some moment.'

The figures were obliterated during the building of the Citadel in the reign of Charles II, but in the excavation the builder turned up perhaps the most concrete proof of all, a great pair of jaws and teeth that could only have belonged to a giant.

SIR FRANCIS DRAKE

To the people of Devon, the doings of Sir Francis Drake were at least as fantastic and extraordinary as Corineus' feats. Although Drake was fêted as a great hero, his triumphs were not attributed to seamanship and bravery alone; both the Spaniards and the British believed he was a wizard who used Supernatural methods. It is said that at his game of bowls, or in some old records 'kales', a form of skittles, Drake tossed the kales logs into Plymouth Sound where each became a fireship and went on to overthrow the Spaniards.

After Drake was knighted and became Lord Mayor of Plymouth, he took his duties to the people he represented very seriously. The laundresses of the city came to him in tears after a long hot summer, complaining that the drought was robbing them of their livelihood. Drake rode up onto Dartmoor, and searched about until he found a spring. He bewitched it with magic incantations and then galloped into town with the stream at the heels of his horse. The corporation with the laundresses at their head met him and led him in triumph into the city. The stream is still visible as Plymouth leat which rises at a morass three miles north of Sheepstor and threads its way down into a reservoir to the north of Plymouth. I always find the first glimpse of the leat a shock, wandering as it does in a neat silvery ribbon, a curious contrast to its surroundings, some of the wildest country on Dartmoor. Even if you accept the rational explanation, it possesses a magical quality that makes the enchantment theory seem more than just a dashing myth.

There are still Devonians who believe that Drake is reincarnated in each succeeding British naval hero, while his accoutrements of war are likewise credited with Supernatural powers. In his poem *Drake's Drum*, Henry Newbolt gave a wider currency to the belief that the drum which hangs at Drake's old home at Combe Sydenham will sound at times of national danger:

> *Take my drum to England. Hang et by the shore,*
> *Strike et when the powder's running low.*

If the dons strike Devon, I'll quit the port of heaven
And drum them up the Channel as I drummed them long ago.

It wasn't only the Spaniards that Drake promised to see off. In the last war, many local people believed that the drum sounded again as strongly as it did in 1588 when the Armada arrived off Plymouth. Others, though, declare scornfully that the only drumming they heard was the thump of the ack-ack guns. Drake's cannonball is also said to roll up and down at Combe Sydenham as a warning of danger, perhaps the same cannonball he used to prove his fidelity in the following story.

When Drake sailed away to circumnavigate the world, he left behind a wealthy fiancée, the daughter of Sir George Sydenham. After three years, her parents persuaded her that he wasn't coming home and arranged to marry her off to a rich merchant. A member of Watchet WI takes up the tale:

'Although 'e'd been gone three years, 'e knew what was happening so at the very door of the chapel, 'e dropped a red-hot cannonball in front of the bridal party. Oh! Give 'en a fright did — and when 'e come home at last 'twas to find 'is bride and 'er dear father a-waiting for 'en with smiles. As for t'other bridegroom, e'd taken isself across the length and breadth of England. But I expect Sir Francis Drake knew where 'e was tew.'

THE DEWERSTONE ROCK

Perhaps because of its barren beauty and isolation, Dartmoor seems to attract the wildest legends of all, many linked to its spectacular outcrops. The Dewerstone Rock near Bickleigh looks to me from a distance more like an eighteenth-century etching of a picturesquely wooded cliff than a real rock. Its name dates back to pre-Christian times, from *Tiues stan*, or rock of Tiue, the Saxon God who also gave his name to Tuesday. The curious monoliths at the summit must have seemed to the credulous heathens, natural altars, the granite chunks etched and eroded into patterns like giant faces. Several

The statue of Sir Francis Drake on Plymouth Hoe. ▶

people have reported seeing blue lights moving among them, winding around the paths, and torchlight processions which disappeared at the approach of humans. Belief in Satanic visitation remains strong and many local people tell of the night, many years ago when the prints of a cloven hoof and a naked human foot were found, climbing to the top. At the edge of a precipitous drop, the human footmarks suddenly ceased but the hoofprints continued down to the river below.

Winter or summer, the bosky hillside has a curiously posed quality, the two streams meeting at its foot foaming like Guinness among the rocks and into dark pools, then rushing under the perfect arches of Shaugh Bridge. The bridge, too, gives a pictorial effect, this time like a gentle vicarage water-colour, the grey span so much at one with the natural landscape that it scarcely seems the work of man. Neither does it seem a typical haunt of the Devil — but here, it is said, the Wild Hunt most often holds its hellish meet before drawing the moorland coverts for its quarry of human souls. On winter nights, the baying of the wild-eyed Wish Hounds echoes through the valley as the hunt moves off in the wake of a tall swarthy figure carrying a hunting-pole. This detail, found in the earliest accounts of the Wild Hunt, reflects the Medieval obsession with the Devil and the tools of his trade:

When I looke into the Fish-ponds in my Garden
Me thinkes I see a thing armed with a rake.

One night the great hunt swept through Shaugh Prior in full cry with the winding of horns and the beating of myriad cloven hooves. Everyone shrank indoors at the unearthly rumble except for one cocky farmer returning home late from the inn, a little the worse for wear. The Devil reined in his headless horse alongside him and the farmer bawled:

'Ho there, Old Nick! What luck with your hunting on the hill? Won't you give me some of your bag?' The Devil smiled a sinister smile and one tooth glinted like a diamond.

'Fresh meat tonight,' he said, 'here, take this.'

Carelessly he tossed him a package wrapped in dock leaves, the size of a lamb's carcase. The farmer unwrapped it greedily, then

◄ **Under the Dewerstone 'two streams meet'.**

reeled back, retching with horror. Inside the dock leaves was the
body of his baby son.

THE TAVISTOCK HARE

The Wild Hunt was not content with human quarry, but often hounded unfortunates beyond the grave. An old Tavistock woman, used
to getting up before the dawn, woke one night at midnight by mis-
take and set off for market. She soon realised her error, for the thunder of the Wild Hunt shook the moorland beneath her and a white
hare, eyes staring, ears flat on its neck, scampered towards her. She
could hear the Wish Hounds howling, a bare two hundred yards behind, but the hare checked its stride and pausing a second, leapt up
onto the pommel of the saddle and into the old woman's lap. She
quickly hid the trembling beast in her pannier and continued on her
way. Next minute, the hounds were around her, leaping and giving
tongue. The Devil's headless horse stamped and reared beside her
own grey mare.
'Tell me, you wrinkled crone, have you seen the white hare we
were chasing? My Wish Hounds followed her scent thus far and no
further.' The old woman shook inwardly and muttered a prayer, but
when she spoke, her voice was steady:
'Oh, no sir. Not a single creature passed this way.' The Devil
swore an oath viler than any human could utter and the Wish Hounds
squirmed on their bellies, trying to flatten themselves into the heather, out of sight of their demonic master. He laid about him with a
great whip of blackened gossips' tongues sewn together and lightning flashed at each crack. Then the whole hellish crew disappeared
over the next hillside, bathed in a sinister blue glow.
The moment they were out of sight, the hare was transformed into
a lovely young girl who said:
'A thousand thanks for saving me from my unenviable fate. I was
condemned to wander Dartmoor, hunted by the Wish Hounds, time
out of mind, until I was able to get behind their tails. If once they had
caught me, my soul would have writhed in torment in the blackest

'The Devil's headless horse reared beside her grey mare.' ▶

'Dartmoor seems to attract the wildest legends . . .'

pit of hell for the rest of eternity. My time on this earth is short, but before I go, I shall grant you a reward in return for your kindness. Your hens shall all lay two eggs instead of one. Your single cow that looks so lean and rickety shall now produce more milk than the biggest herd in the district. But best of all, you shall talk twice as much as before — and although your husband now beats you whenever he comes home the worse for drink, you shall lash him with wit and sarcasm and cow him into submission. From henceforth he shall stand no chance whatever in any matter to be settled by the tongue.'

The beautiful girl became less substantial, her form translucent like a Saint in a stained glass window. Suddenly the old woman caught sight of a group of shining spirits surrounding her. Wonderful music sounded, yet she could hear no recognisable tone or melody, just a wild fanfare like a phalanx of trumpeters, which came, not from any visible instrument but from the mouths of the spirits. The music rose to a splendid crescendo and the troop of spirits bore the young girl up the lightening sky until they faded into a pure silvery haze and were lost from sight. The old woman went home, astonished at what she'd seen and heard and soon discovered that what the girl promised was indeed coming true.

Her stock really did thrive and even the runt of her litter of piglets became a great lean brute of twenty score. After he was slaughtered, she smoked one massive side in her cottage chimney and the prime bacon kept the couple in hearty breakfasts for the whole winter. Now that they no longer lived in squalor, her husband became a changed man. He never again drowned his sorrows in drink, so she had very little occasion to use her newly sharpened tongue on him. Where her new gift did come into its own was at market and ever after, even when she dressed in russet silk and lived in the best house in Tavistock, she managed to haggle the lowest prices of all from the traders. When the gipsy pedlars called round with boxes of ribbons and jewellery, hoping to make an easy killing, they went away amazed, for not once did she ever lose an argument. Indeed she often ended up paying even less for their wares than they'd given in the first place.

SHEEPSTOR

Although the old woman prospered after her brush with the other world, children on Dartmoor are often at risk. East of Yelverton, on Sheepstor stands the Pixies' House, two slanting rocks resting against the vertical side of the tor, 'a critical place for children' after sunset. For some reason, the pixies enjoyed stealing children, although unfortunately only the positively angelic variety, the type that these days gets strangled and left in a ditch to an accompaniment of tear-jerking headlines: ' "She was too good to live", say grieving neighbours.' 'Little angel of Latimer Terrace found murdered.' The catapult and noisy tears brigade could be left beside the house at sunset in perfect safety, as many distracted parents must have found to their cost.

Even in the daylight hours, many people still drop a pin at the house to placate the little people. This perhaps harks back to the belief that the pixies, like the Cornish spriggans or soldier elves, stored great hoards of precious minerals beneath the tors. The grains of gold sometimes found in nearby streams bear this out, while the gift of the pin was perhaps a symbolic addition to the treasure and

mark of respect, just as everyone raises his hat as he passes over the Fairy Bridge between Castletown and Douglas on the Isle of Man. It seems strange that the pixies, so discriminating in their choice of young victims, should accept such comparatively worthless tributes as pins.

The last time I visited Sheepstor, the first snows of the winter lay on its slopes, raked by a biting wind. The only children to be seen romped around pelting one another with snowballs well away from the Pixies' House. I followed their example just in case the Pixies, short of younger quarry, should transfer their attentions to me.

CHOLERA COMES TO SHEEPSTOR

In 1832, the only cholera of the nineteenth century epidemic to reach Sheepstor did so in a roundabout way. A rich Plymouth merchant was stricken and he and his family died one by one. Two unscrupulous brothers visited the house of death in search of anything valuable they could steal, hacking off fingers for the emerald rings they bore, even stripping the man's corpse of its rich satin waistcoat and fine silk shirt. The two thieves quickly gathered a pile of valuables and one foolishly donned the dead man's clothes. As he adjusted his cravat in the looking glass, he saw his brother furtively pocketing a gold watch. He was furious and accused him of trying to take the best of the hoard for himself. Soon the two were at each other's throats and the noise of the fight brought the police to put a stop to the looting.

The two brothers escaped and the one wearing the stolen finery fled to Sheepstor where he hid in a cottage outhouse until the police had gone. He then imposed on the cottagers, pretending to be a rich gentleman who had lost his way on the moors. They believed his story implicitly and took him in as if he were one of the family. Next day he left, warm, well-fed and dressed like a peasant, leaving behind a golden guinea — and the fatal germs of the disease. The peasants lent him a stolid mare and he rode back to Plymouth in comfort. But although he avoided infection, the cottagers died of cholera

◀ Sheepstor: ' . . . the first snows of winter lay on its slopes.'

soon afterwards and only their son survived. Terrified and frantic at the loss of his parents, the lad rode into Tavistock carrying word of the deaths and of the strange events that preceded them. As Sheepstor was famous for its cleanliness and bracing air, the police at once suspected the 'fine gentleman' the boy spoke of, and guessed that he was in fact the thief who'd fled from the Plymouth lawmen. They rode into the city with the youngster and searched until he pointed out his parents' mare and the man who had double-crossed his family with such fatal results. The 'gentleman' was tried and hanged that same week, a punishment the Tavistock police chief declared was 'too merciful by half for such carrion scum'.

LYDFORD LAW

At least in the previous story justice was seen to be done, unlike the sketchy version which prevailed at Lydford Castle until the seventeenth century. This was the Stannary Prison where forest lawbreakers were held while awaiting trial. According to Browne, the Tavistock poet, sentence, even sentence of death, was infinitely preferable to confinement at Lydford:

> *I oft have heard of Lydford law,*
> *How in the morn they hang and draw*
> *And sit in judgment after.*
> *At first I wondered at it much*
> *But then I found the matter such*
> *That it deserves no laughter.*
> *There is a castle on the hill,*
> *I took it for an old windmill,*
> *Its vanes blown off by weather.*
> *To lie therein one night, 'tis guessed,*
> *'Twere better to be stoned or pressed*
> *Or hanged ere thou come thither.*

In spite of a little exaggeration, this is not so far from the truth as you might think. The forest courts operated on a three-tier system

'Death was preferable to imprisonment at Lydford Castle'. ▶

with the man accused of, for example, sheep stealing or grazing in-
fringements brought first before the Court of Attachment. This was
held every forty days by the verderers. If they found him guilty, he
next went to the Court of Swainmote, called three times a year by the
forest freeholders. If they too found the indictment was true, the
man's fate was sealed, although theoretically he had to wait for the
Court of Justice Seat to pass sentence. In practice, since the court
only sat once every three years, the accused was often hanged before
sentence was passed — so that much of the work of the highest court
was done well in advance, and justice was strictly retrospective!

Lydford Castle's bloody reputation continued throughout the sixteenth century and in the reign of Henry VIII, it was described as
'one of the most annoious, contagious and detestable places within
the realm'. Appropriately enough, Hanging Judge Jeffreys presided
there during the Civil War — and although the last execution took
place in 1650, he's still said to haunt the site of the old courtroom in
the shape of a black pig. With so many tales of hauntings by black
dogs, headless horses and the like, the black pig is a welcome
change. All the same, if the real Jeffreys was as black as he's painted, then any self-respecting pig might feel the Judge's reincarna-
tion a real insult to the species.

THE GUBBINGS

Although punishments were indeed harsh and justice unorthodox,
desperate times require desperate measures — and sixteenth-cen-
tury Devon was hardly the law-abiding place it is today. The anti-
quarian Fuller tells in delightfully balanced prose of a Westcountry
Robin Hood, Roger Rowle and his gang of broken men, the Gubbings, who terrorised the district in a less than chivalrous way:

'I have heard of an England beyond Wales, but the Gubbings land
is a Scythia within England. They live in cotts, rather holes than
houses, like swine, and having all in common, multiplied without
marriage into many hundreds.

'Their language is the drosse of the dregs of the vulgar Devonian

'Lydford Gorge seems made for legends . . .' ▶

— and the more learned a man is the worse he can understand them. Their wealth consists in other men's goods and they live by stealing sheep on the More. Living in ignorance of Luxury, the extinguisher of life . . . they hold together like burrs: offend one and all will revenge his quarrel.'

The remnants of the Gubbings lived on until around 1900, providing an eventful and often sinister side to the otherwise even tenor of life round Lydford. The name has survived in colloquial use until now, although most people have forgotten the gang of brigands who used it first. The real meaning of the word has greatly weakened and 'the Gubbings' are now synonymous with 'bits and bobs', 'this and that' or perhaps in Fuller's scornful phrase, 'the drosse of the dregs'.

KIT'S STEPS

Lydford's biggest tourist attraction is its wonderful, sheer gorge, which always reminds me of the description in Coleridge's Kubla Khan:

> *And lo! the deep enchanted cavern which slanted*
> *Down a green hill, athwart a cedarn cover,*
> *A savage spot, as holy and enchanted*
> *As ever 'neath a waning moon was haunted*
> *By woman wailing for her demon-lover.*

The gorge seems made for legends although I know of none about demon lovers.

Kit's Steps are said to commemorate a woman called Old Kitty who slipped and fell to her death on her way home from market. One man who told me about the tradition said that the White Lady of the Water called to her to jump in — and confessed that he often felt the same inexplicable compulsion himself. Some psychologists say that a fear of heights is really the fear of a subconscious desire to throw yourself off, so perhaps the White Lady is just the externalisation of that obscure and terrifying desire within us all.

◀ **Kit's Steps are found in Lydford Gorge.**

In another version, Kitty was a gentlewoman who tried to jump her horse across a narrow chasm in the gorge. On the far side, the horse, perhaps responding to the call of the White Lady, lost his footing, but en route to seemingly certain death on the rocks below, horse and rider lodged in overhanging trees and both lived to leap another day.

THE HUNTED HARE

For all I know, Kitty was part of the hunt that hounded a hare almost to death as the squire tried to prove an old woman guilty of witchcraft. The woman lived with her little grandson, Robin, in appalling poverty near Tavistock. The squire who ran the local pack of harriers used to pay 6d to anyone who told him where a hare was lying on the day of the hunt, a risky business as the offer provided a strong temptation to falsify a sighting, or even catch and then unloose a hare in front of the hounds. One particularly hard winter, the old woman was so close to starvation that she gave in to a blacker temptation still and invoked the powers of darkness in return for the sixpenny piece. It was a coin that meant so little to the squire and so much to her and to Robin, whose little, heart-shaped face was pinched and grey from a diet of rotten potatoes scrounged from the dustbins of richer houses. One Saturday morning when the hunt was meeting at an inn near her cottage, the old woman called Robin to her and said:

'Go and tell the squire you've seen a hare on the high moors above our house.' The little boy was puzzled. How could his Granny have known? She never left her little stool in the kitchen except to go to market. Too hungry to ask too many questions, he trotted off obediently and delivered his message. The hunt moved off in the direction he'd pointed and soon they were in full cry after a large cunning doe who twisted this way and that and eventually plunged into a thicket so dense that even the keenest, most flexible hounds could only stand, forlornly whining and pawing at the wall of thorns. The squire called off the hounds and went to draw another covert, cursing

'. . . a large cunning doe . . . plunged into a thicket . . .' ▶

his bad luck.

The following Wednesday was a lawn meet at a great house, half a mile from the old woman's cottage. Again, she sent Robin off to tell the squire of a hare's whereabouts, this time in a nearby stubble-field. The boy duly received sixpence and the squire growled:

'Here you are, my lad. I only hope we have better sport from your hare this time than we did last.' But it was not to be. The hounds started a hare from almost under their very noses in the thick stubble, but the wily creature doubled back on her tracks and bounded a hundred yards up a stream to throw the hunt off her scent. The squire rode back in a towering rage, swigging liberally at his silver-chased flask of cherry brandy.

'Curse that po-faced urchin — and curse that devilish hare. I could have sworn it was the same one that gave us the slip last Saturday. There is black work afoot — and I smell the stench of witchcraft!'

At the following meet, the squire had enlisted all the able-bodied men in the village to 'help him catch the witch'. Robin again came to report a hare in a little spinney above the town as his grandmother had told him, but before the hounds went in, the squire posted every-one, even the parson, in a great ring round the spinney, so that all means of escape were blocked. Robin walked back to the cottage, watching the preparations, in astonishment. When he got home, his Granny was nowhere to be found and suddenly the truth crystal-lised in his mind. All the little unexplained questions he'd been ask-ing himself fitted together in a flash to produce stone-cold certainty, followed by a slow prickle of fear down his neck. Of course his Granny knew where the hare would be — because she herself was the hare, transformed by one of those strange incantations from the ancient books beneath her bed, the books she said were full of recipes, but which he was always forbidden to touch. In a trice he was up and running as if the Devil were after him, up to the spinney. He was just in time to see a large doe hotly pursued by the hounds, squirming under the hedge and across the field in front of him. For a split second, he raced alongside the hare, urging her on:

'Run Granny, run! Don't let them catch you.' The next moment, his voice was drowned in the din as the pack streamed past him and in the background, he heard the squire's mocking voice:

'Now do you believe me, parson. There's proof that she's a witch. Her own grandson dashes out to watch her torn to pieces. Now she's ours once and for all.'

He spurred on his horse, but the hare, tiring rapidly, made a last spurt and reached the top of the hill above Robin's tumbledown cottage. One hound's teeth ripped a chunk of flesh and fur from her flank but she got free with a desperate wriggle. Down the hill they poured in a solid stream, the hare with her blood-flecked coat and the sinuous hounds on her tail. The hare flung herself inside the open door and disappeared.

'This time she won't escape,' boomed the squire and called off the hounds, 'I'll corner her myself and fling her to the pack.' He strode upstairs, but instead of the hare, he found the old woman, half-dead with exhaustion and bleeding heavily from a deep wound on her leg that corresponded exactly to the bite on the hare's flank.

The squire crossed himself:

'Here parson, do you see the scum of witchcraft. Here she lies with the marks of the black art on her body. Shall we hang her now or drive a stake through her heart at the crossroads?' The old woman gasped in terror.

'Forgive me, but I had no money to buy food for my grandson Robin. I swear that I have never called up the spirits for any other reason but this. Now if I die whatever will come of him?'

'What do I care. He played his part in deceiving me, you evil hag,' snarled the squire in best pantomime baddie style. It was a vein he found difficult as he preferred pressing wild flowers to hunting and ranting at his tenants, but he felt compelled to take up both when he succeeded his father who'd rejoiced in a fearsome reputation. The parson stepped forward.

'Don't judge them too harshly. They only deceived you because they were hungry.'

'Withdraw the plank from your own eye . . .' muttered someone, but subsided as the squire half-turned on him.

'If you pardon them,' continued the parson, 'I give you my word they will never deceive you again. I shall take them into my own house and the old woman can be my housekeeper, while I'll educate the little lad with my own son.' To keep up appearances, the squire snarled at first, but soon gave in. Robin and his Granny moved into the parsonage that very night, and the last thing they did before they left their old home, was to burn the books of witchcraft until nothing was left of them except a pile of ashes and a wisp of smoke.

THE HAT

Anyone who has ever hunted — or worse still hiked across Dartmoor in autumn — will know that the November rains can spell danger, turning low-lying marshland into potentially deadly bogs. Few people are now killed in them but until the drainage schemes of this century they certainly claimed many lives.

Even today, unwary travellers often find out by bitter experience, the true meaning of the Dartmoor word 'stugged' or stuck fast.

Most of the stories about the bogs are fearsome, but a few contain elements of exaggeration and yarning. My favourite tells of Squire Molesworthy who set out to track the River Avon to its source, never an easy task even in summer. The Avon, or Aune, rises near Ryder's Hill and on this occasion, the squire found the going getting heavier and heavier as he plunged about in a treacherous, dismal mire. At each step his feet sunk deeper and deeper in the morass and he was just about to turn back when he saw a tall silk top hat on top of the bog. Wet through and disgusted with his miserable walk, he relieved his feelings by giving the hat a hearty kick. Instead of sailing up into the air, the hat stayed where it was and a gruff voice issued from under it:

'Hi! What be yu'm a-doin' to my hat?'

The squire gasped, 'Is there a man under the hat?'

''Ess, I reckon thur be — and what's more, my hoss is sunken under me as well.'

CHILDE'S TOMB

The moor certainly showed its darker side to one unfortunate traveller, a Saxon lordling called Childe of Plymstock, whom Risdon in his *Survey of Devon* describes as 'a man of fair possessions'. He was overtaken by a Dartmoor snowstorm while he was out hunting. In a desperate effort to prevent himself freezing to death, he killed his beloved horse and disembowelled it, then crept inside its skin for warmth. All this was to no avail and as the wind shrieked louder and the hail drove faster, piercing the sodden carcase, his life ebbed away.

For several days Childe's body lay undiscovered and his disappearance aroused more than the usual interest for he had ordained in his will that all his lands and riches should go to the church where he was eventually buried. Realising he was dying, he had scrawled a laborious message in his horse's blood on a scrap of parchment to remind his executors of their duty:

> 'They fyrste that fyndes and brings mee to my grave,
> The priorie of Plimstoke they shall have.

Four days later, the storm abated and a pedlar crossing the moor caught sight of the body. He stripped it of its rings and gold coins, then continued on to Tavistock where he told his tale:

'A rich man he was, fine clothes — velvet and cloth of gold — but they did him no good, poor fellow. He was stiff as a board, curled up inside his horse's skin.'

The news spread as though on wings and the monks of Tavistock Abbey at once formed a rescue party, intent on bringing back the body they were sure was Childe's and claiming the rich reward. They were not the only ones with this idea. The men of Plymstock considered it was only right that Childe as a local man should be

Childe's Tomb today on Dartmoor.

Part of Tavistock Abbey remaining today.

buried in their Church and they too set out, armed to the teeth on a mission that made a nonsense of the commandment that says 'Thou shalt not covet'. So desperate were they to get the prize for themselves that they were quite prepared to forget a second sacred law into the bargain: 'Thou shalt not kill.' When the Tavistock monks reached the body first, the men of Plymstock cursed and spurred on their horses to the only bridge over the Tavy where they prepared an ambush for the monks to rob them before they reached consecrated ground. But the men of God were too cunning for them and erected 'a slight bridge' across, further upstream, then carried their prize across in triumph. Risdon records how 'the people of Plymstock were deceived by a guile . . . in memory whereof the bridge remains Guilebridge', although many historians now claim that 'guile bridge' is simply a corruption of Guild bridge, that is the one leading to the Guildhall.

The spot on the moor where the body is thought to have been found is marked on the Ordnance Survey maps as Childe's tomb. Even in high summer, its location, the trackless marshy ground between the Swincombe Valley and Fox Tor, is less than appetising. I set out to find Childe's tomb on a wet October Saturday with an adventurous friend, an experienced moor-walker who looked on the wide boggy region we had to cross as just another challenge. We set out from the Old Whiteworks near Princetown, across the valley from Fox Tor. From a distance the ground looked like a plushy green carpet but when we reached it, I soon found out why it was marked on our map as Fox Tor Mires. Little streams and rivulets threaded their way through the landscape, oozing into peaty pools and welling up at each step from under even the thickest piles of reeds. Most terrifying of all was my encounter with a quaking mire, a virulently green patch of grass which shivered at every reluctant step I took, as it was literally floating on a broad expanse of muddy water. At one stage, my foot plunged in with a sickening squelch, filling my wellington with water, but even this seemed a small price to pay to reach the other side safely. The so-called footpath, marked with painted stakes is not to be recommended in autumn. The rains pay no attention to man-made tracks and the stakes seem designed to lead you straight into the boggiest tracts of all. But despite the privations we suffered, we could at least plot our progress on a map and had the benefit of the gently greying daylight to find our way back, however tortuously. On the wild night that Childe met his end, Fox Tor must have seemed as bleak as Siberia. A hewn granite cross now marks the site and although this dates back only 90 years, Risdon records that some form of monument commemorating Childe's death stood on the moor in the seventeenth century. Beneath the cross are the remains of a barrow and stone cist within a stone circle, but historians say that these are older than Tavistock Priory itself, which was founded in the tenth century. In spite of this, the memorial could well have stood here, as Christians in the Middle Ages often erected crosses on older pagan monuments.

The couplet which promised the 'priorie of Plimstoke' to whoever found Childe's body is a fabrication, since there never was a priory at Plymstock. All the same, Risdon in 1630 assured his readers that 'these verses were once to be read' on the monument. Thirty years later, Fuller gives a different version:

> He that finds and brings me to my tomb
> The land of Plimstock shall be his doom.

With so many contradictions, and variations on a theme, theories about Childe's identity and the truth behind the legend abound. My favourite suggests that Childe really existed, in the guise of a noble called Ordulf. His name first crops up in charters around 1044 and he was still living in 1066 when he appeared in the Domesday Book as lord of nineteen manors in Devon, two in Cornwall and one in Somerset. In *Devonshire Studies*, the authors identify Ordulf as the gigantic son of a lord called Ordgar. Father and son were both buried in Tavistock Abbey and Ordulf's sepulchre became one of the sights of the place because it was so enormous. In 1125 William of Malmesbury described Tavistock Abbey and gave an account in Latin of Ordulf's (or Edelfus') feats:

'He was travelling to Exeter in company with King Edward his kinsman. On dismounting from their horses at the city gate, they found the door doubly bolted and barred against them. Thereupon, Edelfus seized the bolts with both hands and with very little apparent effort broke them to pieces, tearing down part of the wall as he did so. Then warming to the work and gnashing his teeth, he gave a second proof of his strength. Loosening the gate with a kick, he forced open the hinges on either side with such violence as to shiver the door posts. The rest of the company applauded but the king pretended to make light of it, saying he must be possessed of the Devil's own strength.

40

'He gave another remarkable display of prowess in a wood near Horton in Dorset, where there is a monastery, now destroyed, which thanks to his generosity ranked in those days as an abbey. To this place, he used to resort in moments of leisure. There down a ravine which abounds in game, a stream flows ten feet wide. Edelfus used to bestride this and with a small knife, using slight and almost nugatory strokes, would strike off the heads of the beasts of chase that were driven towards him so that they fell in the water.

'For all his size and strength he died in the prime of life (the literal translation from the Latin being 'in the heat of his prime') leaving instructions that he was to be buried at Horton. But as he had directed certain legacies to be given to the church with his body, his wishes were frustrated by the violence of Abbot Sihtric, who carried off both gifts and giver to his own monastery Tavistock. Later on, under king William, Sihtric turned pirate, to the disgrace of his order and the discredit of his church.'

If you compare the story of Childe with the account of Ordulf's death, there are so many resemblances that they seem to be two versions of the same tale. Both men are rich landowners, fond of hunting, who meet a premature end. Although the cause of Ordulf's death is not recorded, the phrase 'in the heat of his prime' is both ironic and poignant when you remember that Childe froze to death.

The difference between the two names is easy to explain. In the eleventh century, the Old English word *cild*, the ancestor of 'child' was used as a title of honour, then and throughout the Middle Ages, as in Childe Roland. Although we know little of the exact social status of these 'Children', they were not children in the modern sense, but probably men of high rank, therefore Childe's full title could well have been Childe Ordulf.

As Ordulf meets his end near Tavistock, his remains would certainly be buried there, rather than be carried to Dorset, whatever instructions he gave while he was alive. The legacy, promised to Horton Abbey was in line with established custom. Although a certain church, Tavistock Abbey in this case, would have legal rights to a due known as soul-scot at the death of a local lord, the noble could promise a gift to another church i.e. Horton Abbey if he wanted to be buried there instead.

This sort of bequest must often have led to legal wrangling and if so, the church with possession of the body would have a strong case to collect all the fees and legacies particularly if it already had prior claim to soul-scot, a striking example of possession being nine parts of the law. This time, Tavistock hit the jackpot while Horton lost out and was destroyed within fifty years, perhaps because of its lost revenues.

The story definitely gives the lie to the common misconception that all Medieval monks were saintly and unworldly creatures. Running a large, costly foundation like Tavistock was a cut-throat business, very much a case of the survival of the fittest, and the Abbot Sihtric, who according to William of Malmesbury later became a pirate, was obviously well-suited to either vocation. In his book *Worthies of England*, Fuller tells the story of Childe and then reflects: 'They must rise early, yea not sleep at all, who over-reach monks in matter of profit.'

To me, the Childe legend has so obviously evolved from the account of Ordulf's life and death, that it is more than just another example of the wiliness of monks. The power-struggle which comes to light through historical research into customs and documents of the time is exactly mirrored in the drama of the bloody couplet and fruitless ambush on the Tavy. It is this mirroring that makes the legend of Childe an almost perfect example of folklore based on fact.

FITZ'S WELL

Not everyone who got lost on the moor met the same sad end as Childe. In the sixteenth century John Fitz of Fitzford and his lady were pixy-led and wandered for days without food or drink, convinced that they would starve or freeze to death. Just as they were giving up hope, they heard a faint trickle and looking down, saw a tiny spring. The two knelt to drink, praising God as they did so, and the timely mouthfuls of water gave them the strength they needed to stagger on to the nearest cottage. John Fitz was so overjoyed at their miraculous deliverance that he raised a stone above the little spring to mark it for other benighted travellers and perhaps save their lives as his had been saved. The stone remains to this day, inscribed with his initials I.F. and the date 1568. It is marked on the Ordnance Survey map as Fice's Well, a corruption of Fitz's, and lies near the Blackabrook about a mile north of Dartmoor Prison. If you visit the well, strong boots or wellingtons are a necessity as the ground round the Blackabrook is often boggy. I also recommend the largest scale map of the area you can buy, as on my first expedition in search of the well, I failed to find it because my map wasn't detailed enough.

THE HAIRY HANDS OF POSTBRIDGE

These days, you would think that the car and the motor-bike had taken all risks out of moorland travel. After all you stand no chance of being pixy-led at the wheel, and however bad the storm you can always shelter in a lay-by until it passes without any likelihood of freezing to death. All the same, a bridge on the main road near Postbridge is famous for a horrifying phenomenon which singles out the drivers of motor vehicles for its unwelcome attentions.

A large pair of hairy hands suddenly appears on the driving wheel or handlebars and wrenches the car or motor-cycle off the road and into the ditch. Although several of the drivers have escaped physically unhurt, all have been found literally gibbering with fear and swearing that despite their frantic struggles, they were utterly powerless to wrest the wheel from the terrible hands which disappeared as soon as their evil work was done.

People, especially those from up-country, are inclined to scoff at the legend and suggest more mundane reasons, not unconnected with the excellent local hostelries, for the spate of crashes. Others blame the camber of the road at that point, but neither explanation can account for the terrible feeling of dread immediately before the hands' appearance, a feeling which all the victims, even those knowing nothing of the tradition, claim they've experienced. A Somerset doctor who ended up with his car on its side in the ditch three years ago told me he now believed implicitly that some malignant force had sent it out of control.

'The atmosphere inside the car suddenly became deathly cold and I had a feeling almost like paralysis. I stopped the car and found I was trembling all over but I could think of no rational explanation for it. I'd had nothing to drink and as far as I knew I was perfectly healthy. Well, in a couple of minutes the feeling passed off and I drove on, but after about two hundred yards it came back worse than ever. Although I didn't see anything specific I was aware of a great weight or force inside the car, something quite out of my control. The

steering wheel seemed to go wild and it was wrenched out of my hands. The car skidded right across the road and next second I was hanging from my seat belt. It was terrifying and quite inexplicable — and I know I didn't imagine that feeling I had before. Some people ask me if I got mildly concussed in the crash and dreamed up the whole business, but I was conscious the whole time and I didn't have a single bruise.'

After hearing sober accounts like that, I like to believe that the hairy hands or at least some alien phenomenon exists, perhaps a horse-loving spirit who abhors the internal combustion engine and all its works. One thing is for certain, whenever I'm driving home in the Postbridge direction late at night, I always give the main road a wide berth, going several miles out of my way to avoid it. If I have passengers in the car, I generally think up a harmless ruse to explain the detour as I don't want to be accused of superstition when I'm just being careful!

Near Postbridge: the bridge where the 'hairy hands' have taken control of vehicles, forcing them off the road.

WIDECOMBE IN THE MOOR

Like Postbridge, Widecombe has experienced a phenomenon which people are still trying to explain. In this case, the occurrence is far less recent than the hairy hands. It happened on Sunday 21 October 1638 while the Reverend George Lyde was taking the afternoon service. A terrible thunderstorm swept down the valley and centred on Widecombe Church.

In the words of a contemporary account: 'There was terrible and fearful thunder like the noise of many guns, accompanied by dreadful lightning, to the great amazement of the people, the darkness still increasing that they could not see each other. Then an extraordinary flame passed right through the church, filling it with a loathsome smell, like brimstone and a great ball of fire fell through the roof.' The whole congregation dropped to the floor, terror-struck, as a large beam crashed down between the parson and his clerk. Neither man was hurt but it was a different story in the rest of the church where four people were killed and 62 injured.

Many of the congregation pleaded, 'Shall we go from the church before the fire from heaven consumes us all?' But the parson was firm: 'Let us make an end of prayer. It were better that we died here than in another place.' He looked at one strangely scorched and withered beam alight with blue and green flames and it reminded him forcibly of the fires of hell. He finished his prayers and took stock of the disaster in which the lightning seemed curiously selective.

According to Mrs Bray: 'The parson's wife was scorched but her child seated by her in the same pew received no injury. A woman who attempted to rush out was so miserably burnt that she expired that night. Many persons likewise in a few days after died from the same cause.'

In an early account 'another man had his head cloven, his skull rent into three pieces and his brains thrown on the ground whole, but the hair of his head, through the violence of the blow stuck fast to a pillar near him where it remained a woeful spectacle a long while after.'

Widecombe: 'an extraordinary flame passed through the church.' ▶

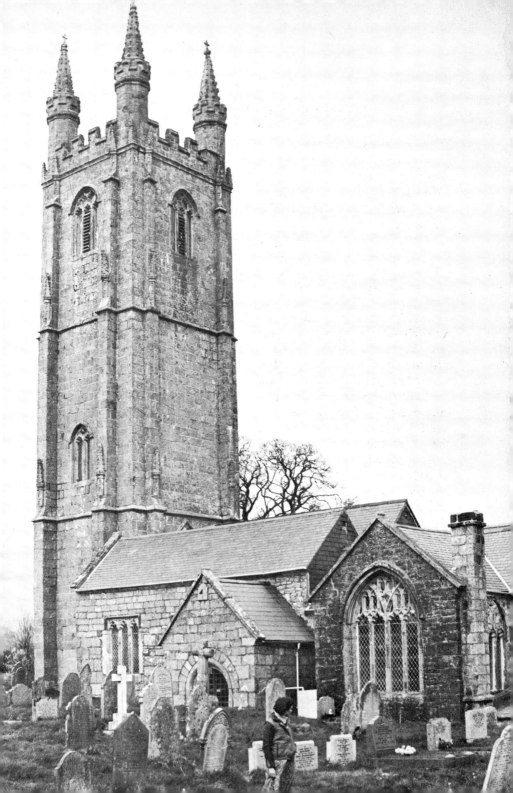

Richard Hill, the village schoolmaster of the time, described the 'woeful spectacle' in jog-trot verses which now hang in the Church, inscribed on four wooden boards. He was particularly impressed with the miraculous deliverance of so many of the congregation and the way the lightning seemed quite arbitrary in its choice of victim:

One man was scorched so that he lived but fourteen days and died
Whose clothes were very little burnt, but many there beside
Were wounded scorched and stupefied in that so strange a storm
Which who had seen would say 'twas hard to have preserved a
worm,
Now what we here related have in truth in most men's mouths.
Some had their skin all over scorched but no harm in their clothes
One man had money in his purse which melted was in part
A key likewise that hung thereto, and yet the purse not hurt,
Save only some black holes so small as with a needle made.
Lightning some say no scabbard hurts, but breaks and melts the
blade.
Amongst the rest a little child which scarce knew good from ill
Was seen to walk amidst the Church and yet preserved still.
The greatest admiration was that most men should be free
Among so many dangers here which we did hear and see.

The poem ends with the inevitable moral:

All ye that look upon these lines of this so sad a story,
Remember who hath you preserved, ascribe unto His glory
The preservation of your lives, who might have lost your breath
When others did, if mercy had not step'd 'twixt you and death.
We hope that they were well prepared, although we know not how
'Twas then with them, it's well with you if you are ready now.
Amos IV, 11: "Ye were as a firebrand plucked out of the burning."

Although Richard Hill evidently considered the disaster an act of God, the superstitious element was convinced it knew better: after all why should God want to destroy His house? Surely, few of the Widecombe congregation could really be called too good for this world — and if they were, why not the parson? No, this was obviously the work of the Devil. At once rumours began flying around

'. . . the liquor hissed as it went down his throat.' ▶

and soon a wealth of evidence built up to prove that the devastation was in fact the work of Satan come to claim his own.

Twenty years earlier, a wild young bachelor of the parish, known as Widecombe Jan had made a pact with the Devil in the careless way that so many youths, particularly Devonians, were wont to. Perhaps it was a form of natural selection, which these days has been superseded by the perilous craze for motor-bikes. In the legends, at least, almost everyone who has any truck with Old Nick comes to a sticky end — and Jan's was stickier than most. He had promised the Devil he could have his soul if he ever found him asleep in church, thinking there was little chance of this happening, what with the hard pews and the pretty servant girls to flirt with. On that October Sunday, though, Jan was feeling rather frayed round the edges. He'd been to the inn the night before and had drunk and caroused to the early hours before staggering home at three, carolling most unorthodox versions of the hymns he was now trying to mouth without splitting his head open. His eyes started to droop during the Collect, and by the time the parson started on his sermon, he was snoring merrily with his mouth open.

That morning, a tall swarthy stranger passing through Poundsgate stopped at the Tavistock Inn to ask the way to Widecombe. The landlady gave him directions and offered him a drink. The stranger accepted civilly enough but when he smiled, the landlady caught sight of a row of uneven fangs. Highly suspicious by this time, she noticed that the liquor hissed as it went down his throat. Worst of all, from her point of view, although the stranger paid for his pint with a purse of red gold, the moment he was out of sight the money turned to dry leaves. One woman at least knew who was riding for Widecombe.

On his arrival, the Devil tethered his horse to one of the Church pinnacles and dropped through the roof in the ball of fire. Seizing Widecombe Jan, he threw him violently against a pillar, dashing his brains out, while the storm raged throughout the rest of the church, diverting everyone's attention from what was going on. Satan dragged Jan's body to the top of the tower, making sure he had tight hold of his soul into the bargain, and as he unloosed his horse, he overthrew the pinnacle which toppled into the church causing greater damage still. Then in true Demon King style, he vanished amid thunder and lightning and a great puff of green smoke.

Not surprisingly, pacts with the Devil seemed to lose popularity in

the Widecombe area after this date but the advent of the motor-bike
has kept the population within manageable bounds; I found this to
my cost when I narrowly avoided a lemming-like biker who met me
on the wrong side of the road as he shot over the brow of the hill at
70 mph. I suppose the one advantage of the new method is that it
causes less full-scale destruction and far fewer innocent people stand
to meet a violent end now than on that fateful October day in 1638.

OLD CROCKERN 'ISSELF

Not content with Satanic visitations, the moor possesses its own
familiar spirit, Old Crockern, who represents to many local people
the force which lies beneath the bleak and inscrutable landscape. A
rich Manchester farmer visited Dartmoor and decided that it was
ripe for cultivation, so he moved to Devon and set about enclosing
and farming the land in the very shadow of Crockern Tor. He soon
became unpopular because of his high-handed ways and grabbing
nature. Like many self-made men, his behaviour caused people to
wonder why he'd made himself like that, but he was as thick-skinned
as he was boorish and took no notice of hints on how he might ingratiate himself with his neighbours.

One day, he met the local simpleton lying in the heather near the
new enclosures, humming quietly to himself: and scratching his ear
with a stick.

'How now master,' mumbled the idiot, 'there be summat I must
tell ye. I dreamed I falled asleep and I zeed the very spirit of the
moor.' Twas Old Crockern 'isself. Grey he was, like granite, with
eyes set deep in his head, eyes like them pools of peat-water. He
rumbled in his heathery beard and then roared like thunder: "If he
scratches my back, I'll tear his pockets out." I know 'twas you he
meant, master, because his great grey hand rested on all yon parcel
of moor. Take my advice, master and don't you cross him. I've heard
Old Crockern is a mighty powerful fellow when his dander's up.'

The farmer laughed, 'You great slobbering idiot! Don't come to
me with your half-baked, bug-a-boo stories. Don't you know there's
no such person as Crockern? To my mind, there's far too much superstitious nonsense talked round here and far too little good hard
work. No wonder the farmers only eke a bare living from the land and

everyone looks lantern-jawed like the very picture of hunger.'

He patted his own well-filled stomach contentedly. 'In no time, I'll have that land making me a second fortune, so tell that to your precious Crockern.'

Whatever the idiot told him, Crockern must have been unimpressed, for the farmer's grandiose plans folded like a house of cards: he soon found he could neither drain the bogs nor farm the granite and the more he spent the less return he got. Within two years his purse was drained dry and instead of making a second fortune, he had squandered all his capital. So the idiot's prophecy was indeed fulfilled; Crockern was true to his word and tore the farmer's pockets out and the wretched man spent the rest of his days in the workhouse.

JAY'S GRAVE

Until well into this century, only one group ranked below paupers in the social scale, unmarried mothers, and any working-class girl who found she was pregnant had little to look forward to except a lifetime of institutions and moral condemnation of herself and her child. A serving-maid who worked at a great house near Widecombe was seduced by her master's student son and when she confessed that she was expecting a baby, she was driven from the house in disgrace. Destitute, with nowhere to go, and out of her mind with shame and guilt, the unfortunate girl drowned herself in a pond little more than three feet deep. When her body was discovered, she was buried like all suicides in unconsecrated ground.

Her grave lies beside the road half a mile north of Hound Tor and it is marked on Ordnance Survey maps as Jay's grave. All the same, no-one is quite sure whether Jay was her christian name, surname or initial since some people believe her name was Mary Jay, others that the initial J stood for Jane. Whoever she was, she is certainly not forgotten, for there are always fresh flowers on her grave, although no-one has ever been found leaving them there.

The last time I stopped to look, a tiny vase contained sprigs of

◀ ''Twas Old Crockern 'isself'.

bright berries and a posy of marigolds and nasturtiums while on the headstone lay a small heap of coins. I fished in my pocket and added a few coppers to the pile, hoping that it was destined for some present-day traveller down on his luck, and perhaps as desperate as that unknown servant-girl when she decided to take her own life.

STEPHEN'S GRAVE

Unwanted pregnancy provided a strong inducement to young women to commit suicide. Among young men, the motive was often betrayal in love and this was what happened to George Stephens, a farm-labourer of Peter Tavy parish. He was betrothed to a beautiful girl and was so desperately in love that he could hardly wait for his wedding day. At night he used to wander up and down outside her

**'There are always fresh flowers on Jay's Grave' (left)
which lies half a mile north of Hound Tor (below).**

cottage in the hope of seeing her shadow against the curtains.

The week before the wedding, he discovered that she was playing him false with his best friend and he went almost mad with grief and rage. Controlling his features as well as he could, he went on, seemingly as if nothing had happened but gradually a plan formed in his mind. He took a great rosy apple and immersed it in indetectable poison. Soon, enough had soaked in to kill a garrison, so he took it round to his sweetheart who accepted it with a false smile, took one bite and died in agony on the spot. George made his way back home and, practical to the last, fed the pigs, before swallowing the rest of the poison. At the second of his death, white linen lying out to bleach was caught up into the air — a symbol of his spirit's release. Like Mary Jay, he could not be buried in consecrated ground and was laid to rest beneath an unmarked stone on the border of Peter Tavy parish. The stone is still visible up on the moor above the village, a marker on one of my favourite rides and a real conversation piece, as whoever I'm riding with comes up with a different version of the tragic tale.

BOWERMAN'S NOSE

A short walk from Jay's Grave on Hayne Down, near Manaton, stands one of Dartmoor's best-loved landmarks, Bowerman's Nose. The weathered granite formation is unmistakeable, for seen from one angle it resembles the profile of a man with a huge bulbous nose like two potatoes, rearing forty feet above the boulders and outcrops scattered over the slope. As usual the etymologists have a stuffy explanation for the origin of its name, claiming that Bowerman is a corruption of the Celtic *veor maen* or great stone. I prefer the local version, that a man called Bowerman lived at Hound Tor around 1066 and sported a nose identical to the splendidly stubby organ that still adorns the granite column.

The Author at Bowerman's Nose: '. . . it resembles the profile of a man with a huge bulbous nose.' ▶

THE FAIRY OINTMENT

From noses, now, to eyes and a tale from Holne on the south side of the moor where a renowned midwife named Morada lived alone. One night she cowered in bed during a terrific storm when she heard an insistent knocking from downstairs. She ignored the noise for ten minutes but it grew louder and louder until the knocking almost broke the shutters. She threw open the window and saw a rider on a great horse below.

'My wife is ill,' he gasped desperately, 'you must come down at once to save her.' The old woman was terrified of the strange fierce man.

'What, on a night like this? I wouldn't come if she was the Queen of Fairyland herself.'

'But you must. It's a matter of life or death.' He produced a leather purse. 'Look, I'll pay you ten gold guineas if you'll come,' and he counted out the glittering coins in his palm. Morada's eyes glistened and her fear evaporated. She noticed that the man was beautifully dressed in silks and velvets and spoke in a pure, musical voice like the song of a thrush.

'Very well, I'll go with you,' she declared. The rider was overjoyed and promised to pay her five guineas at once and the rest once her job was done.

'Now you must do all I say,' he warned, 'and no harm will come to you. Put away the coins and I'll blindfold you.' Morada did as she was told and he lifted her up behind him on the saddle. Next minute, they were galloping like the wind over the moor, turning this way and that so that she soon lost all sense of where they were going. They reached a gracious house and once inside, the man took off her blindfold and led her into an exquisite room where a dainty little lady lay asleep.

'This is my wife,' he said, lighting the silver lamps beside the bed. As you can see, she is not mortal, but a fairy princess. She has been banished from fairyland for a year because she has married me, her cousin. We return in three weeks, but in the meantime, I need your

◀ **'The prince punched her hard in the left eye.'**

help to deliver our baby safely. Take this ointment and once the child is born, rub it on its eyelids.'

The nurse took the little jar of opalescent film and forgot about it until the drama of the birth was over. The lady had an adorable little boy, tiny but perfect and pink and white, a world away from the creased, crimson bawlers so many human mothers produce. It was then Morada remembered the ointment and gently smoothed it onto the child's eyelids where it disappeared miraculously as soon as it touched the silken skin. Curiously, she touched her left eyelid with it and felt a pleasant tingling sensation and nothing more.

All too soon, the three weeks were up and the fairy prince carried her back home, just as she had come. True to his word, he paid her the rest of the money and turned to wave as he galloped away. Next morning she awoke to a strange world. Her bed seemed huge, the table a vast plateau, the cat as big as a pony and she could see the moon and stars as well as the sun. Then she remembered the ointment and closed her left eye. Immediately everything returned to normal and she realised that she had forgotten to give back the pre-

Dartmoor ponies.

cious jar. She heard hoofbeats and saw the rider returning, so she scurried outside and dropped a deep curtsey:

'My lord, I still have your ointment, I . . .'

'What, can you see me?' he thundered, 'With which eye?'

'The left one,' she faltered. 'I didn't know I'd done anything wrong.' The prince punched her hard in the left eye and everything returned to its normal size.

'Give me back the box,' he ordered. 'That ointment allowed you to see with the vision of a fairy and none of our secrets would have been safe, so I've blinded your left eye as a punishment. It's a pity, as my wife was very fond of you, and here's her parting gift.' He dropped ten more guineas in her lap.

Despite the loss of her eye, Morada consoled herself with her new-found wealth, more than she had ever owned in her life before. She lived in comfort for the rest of her days but she never saw the fairy folk again.

THE WEAVER OF DEAN COMBE

A few miles south of Holne lies the hamlet of Dean Combe and it was here that a weaver of great fame and skill, called Knowles, lived all his life. He was a hard-working man who enjoyed his well-earned prosperity but he still spent long hours at his loom up to the day he died. Old habits die hard and the next day, he appeared at the loom in his chamber, working as hard as he'd done in life. His son was appalled and called in the parson to exorcise his father's spirit.

'Knowles,' shouted the vicar, 'come down, this is no place for thee.'

'I will,' replied the ghost, 'as soon as I have worked out my quill.'

But the parson was insistent: 'Nay, thou hast been long enough at thy work. Come down at once.' He took a handful of earth, and muttering a prayer, he walked upstairs and threw it in the ghost's face. Knowles uttered a great howl and in a second he was transformed into a black hound.

'Now you will follow me to the gate of the wood,' commanded the parson sternly, as if to a naughty dog, 'and you will walk at my heel to the Hound's pool where I have a task that will keep you busy for eternity.' The two reached the wood and a great wind sprang up, bending the trees on either side of them with a noise like the parting of oceans. At the brink of the Hounds' Pool, the parson found a nutshell with a hole in it.

'Take this shell,' he ordered, 'and when you have emptied the whole pool with it, you can rest, but not before.' The hound's ears drooped and he looked up at the parson mournfully but to no avail. It is said that you can still hear him on winter nights, howling at his task until the end of time.

CRANMERE POOL

The theme of an impossible task as a punishment is common in legends, ranging from the classical myths of Sisyphus and his uphill work with the boulder and the labours of Hercules to the local lore of Tregeagle vainly striving to empty Dozmary Pool with a leaking limpet shell and the black hound with his nutshell with a hole in it.

Another spirit who suffered a similar fate had once been a rich miller and Mayor of Okehampton into the bargain. His name was Benjamin Gayer but everyone knew him as Bingie and when he returned to his old haunts after his death, he was confined to Cranmere Pool, a bleak spot high up among the tors of northern Dartmoor. Bingie was condemned to drain the boggy pool with an oat sieve, but far from despairing or trying to escape as Tregeagle did, he set his fertile brain to solve the problem. One day he found a sheepskin on the moor and spread this across the bottom of the sieve, which so improved its efficiency that he baled out all the water and drowned Okehampton town.

The population were horrified, not to mention the clergy who had originally banished him to Cranmere, for his spirit was once again free to roam the town and terrorise the local people. The Archdeacon summoned a posse of twenty-four parsons who in turn called on the errant spirit in different languages to leave the town in peace. All their pleas had no effect until the twenty-fourth conjured Bingie in Arabic. For some reason, this did the trick; perhaps he'd always meant to give himself up but wanted to hear all the different tongues first, anyway he turned into a black colt and allowed himself to be bridled and ridden back to Cranmere. The moment his rider loosed the bridle, the colt plunged into the pool and now haunts the area,

'The legends have become part of the Dartmoor landscape.'

whinnying in frustration, for it is such a desolate and dangerous place to reach that only a handful of the hardiest walkers make the trek. They of course are a great disappointment to an ambitious ghost as they're far too stolid and nerveless to show the slightest hint of fear even when the colt materialises in front of their noses.

THE WHITE BIRD OF THE OXENHAMS

Not all apparitions are as harmless and amiable as Bingie. They sometimes act as a premonition of death and many appear to members of a particular family. The best-documented example of this is the Oxenham family from South Zeal which is haunted at times of death by a white bird.

The tradition dates back centuries to the time of Margaret Oxenham who was heiress to a rich estate. She was due to be married to a local landowner called Bertram but, a few weeks before the wedding, he was hit on the head and became an imbecile who did little but roam the east wing of his parents' mansion, like the mad woman in Jane Eyre.

Margaret was at first inconsolable but later consented to marry Sir John of Roxamcave. As the bride and her attendants made their way up the aisle, the guests noticed a white bird hovering over her head but it disappeared soon afterwards and the service proceeded. Just as the priest was about to ask the binding questions, there was a commotion at the back of the church and mad Bertram rushed to the altar, throwing off all restraint with the strength of ten, and stabbed the bride to death. As she died, the white bird flew through the church and out of the west door.

The first historical record of the white bird came just before the death of Grace Oxenham in 1618 and twenty-three years later, her son James published a tract setting out the circumstances of recent deaths within his family. His son John, aged 21, died suddenly two days after a bird with a white breast had appeared in his room and hovered over the bed. Five days later James's wife, Thomasin, fell ill, saw the white bird and died. Soon afterwards, the same thing happened to her little sister Rebecka and her infant daughter.

James Howell in *Familiar Letters*, 1646 claims he saw in a London stone mason's a marble slab about to be sent to Devonshire with an inscription that: 'John Oxenham, Mary his sister, James his son and Elizabeth his mother had each the appearance of such a bird fluttering about their beds as they were dying.'

The white bird was still faithful and active up to 1873 when a Mr G.N. Oxenham died in Kensington. His nephew, the Reverend Henry Oxenham claimed that Supernatural flutterings were heard in the dying man's chamber and that, a week before the death, his daughter and a friend who knew nothing of the tradition heard a commotion outside. They opened a window and saw a strange white bird considerably larger than a pigeon perched on a bush outside. Some workmen were trying to drive it away by throwing their hats at it. It must have been quite a come-down for the creature that once inspired shudders as the aristocratic harbinger of doom to be mocked and assaulted by tipsy artisans, so it is no wonder that despite a long and distinguished history of successful hauntings, it hasn't been seen since.

THE CANDLE OF MARWOOD

Throughout the Devon legends, the spirits of the dead can take many forms, as can the Devil himself, and he generally uses his powers of transformation for distinctly sinister ends. Luckily for them, most Devonians seem well aware of the threat and take effective action against it.

The mother of a servant-girl named Mary, who lived at Marwood near Barnstaple, was a typical country-woman, a devout church-goer who constantly warned her daughter of her duties and her short-comings. Mary was a normal young girl with her head full of whom she should marry and one day she took a prayer-book and glanced through the Marriage service on a Sunday.

'For pity's sake, Mary,' shrieked her mother, 'don't read that before your wedding-day — if you do, you'll never be married except in the churchyard.'

Mary sulkily put the book down: 'That's just superstition, mother. Whatever difference can it make?' She took up a pair of nail-scissors and started to cut her nails sullenly.

Her mother exploded: 'Mary! How many times have I told you that rhyme: 'Who on the Sabbath pares his horn, Twere better he had ne'er been born.'

'Oh, you're impossible, nothing in your head except a pack of silly old rhymes and old wives tales,' flounced Mary. 'I'm going for a walk'. Her mother took a breath — 'And don't tell me not to talk to strangers.'

Once outside, her temper cooled in the chill air and she stepped out briskly, her dark curls bouncing as she walked. On the edge of the wood, she met a handsome stranger and disregarding her mother's warning she chatted to him in a friendly way and even agreed to see him the following night. Her mother of course was horrified.

'Tell me quickly, child, was he dark or fair and did he have a cloven hoof? It could even be Old Nick you're walking out with, you shameless little madam.'

'He was dark, mother, and he wore a funny old boot on one foot.'

This fully aroused her mother's suspicions and she visited the priest who confirmed that this must indeed be the Devil trying to take her daughter for his own. He gave the woman strict instructions what to do and she went home armed with a candle.

The following night, the stranger came to the door and asked if Mary was ready to come with him. Her mother stood in the doorway with a lighted candle and asked him to wait outside, saying the girl would come as soon as the candle burned down. Then she hastened out of the back door, across the croft to the church where the priest was waiting. She snuffed out the candle and the two of them walled it up in a secret recess behind the rood-screen.

Meanwhile, the girl was watching the stranger through the cottage windows, hidden behind the curtains, torn between fear of the misshapen foot and admiration for her fine friend. But at exactly the second the last brick was laid to wall up the candle, he disappeared in a burst of blue flame. Mary's mother breathed a deep sigh of relief but the priest warned her against complacency:

'If ever the candle shall be taken from its niche and burned, your daughter's soul will be snatched by the Prince of Evil, even though she were in the bliss of Paradise.'

THE DEVIL'S STONE AT SHEBBEAR

If the next legend is true, then Mary's soul looks pretty safe, for the Devil's bones are said to be buried beneath a great stone on the green at Shebbear. The stone is turned every year on 5 November after a religious service around it and a long jangle of bells. The local people say this is to prevent the Devil getting his rest. He certainly seems to need his sleep and make full use of unbroken slumbers for the ceremony was not held one autumn during the First World War and the next year was utterly disastrous for the village and nearby farms. Many local men were lost in the fighting and the harvest

'. . . she hastened across the croft to the church where the priest was waiting.' ▶

failed on a grand scale. The stone weighs about a ton and the handful of men, despite little formal physics teaching, who turn it each year with crowbars know almost instinctively exactly where to lever and where to exert force for maximum effect. After centuries of shifting great stones for building walls and houses, this knowledge seems bred into succeeding generations of local families.

The ceremony itself probably originated from pagan rites, for the stone was there long before Shebbear Church was built and the tale of the Devil's bones sounds like the invention of Christian moralists. All the same the ritual could well have been designed to drive away evil spirits. It certainly provides some excitement in the bleakest part of the year, whichever gods you worshipped and it only needed a Christian gloss to make it acceptable to members of the new Faith.

◀ Marwood Church — ' . . . he disappeared in a burst of blue flame.'
St Michael's Church at Brentor — 'no cars can reach the summit.' ▼

St Michaels' Church, Brentor — The villagers continually rebuilt the Church at the bottom of the hill 'but each time, Old Nick carried it back to the crown of the tor . . .'

BRENTOR

The remarkable church perched on the top of Brentor demands high standards of fitness from its congregations, not to mention its brides and pall-bearers for no cars can make their way to the summit and everyone, unless they are being carried in a wooden waistcoat, has to get there on foot. Like Shebbear this, too, suffered a Satanic visitation and the church's awkward if striking position is attributed to the Devil. It was first built at the bottom of the hill and dedicated to St Michael, but the Devil, jealous of the Saint's power, removed it to the summit. The villagers continually rebuilt it on its original site but each time, Old Nick carried it back to the crown of the tor, and used it for his own black ends.

Eventually the villagers gave up trying to rebuild it but appealed to St Michael to come and drive out his old adversary. He consented and after a tremendous wrestling match, he got the upper hand and kicked the Devil down the hill, tossing a great boulder after him to help him on his way. Today both St Michael's Church and the great boulder still stand on Brentor, enduring monuments to the power of God over Evil.

THE HUBBLESTONE

For the people of North Devon, evil took both demonic and human forms and in the eighth and ninth centuries, no village was safe from Viking raids. But the pirates did not always triumph and on at least one occasion, the Devonians put up spirited resistance. In the reign of Alfred the Great, a Danish leader called Hubba landed near the village of Appledore with a fleet of thirty-three ships. He and his men besieged nearby Kenwith Castle which was on the site now known as Henny Castle to the north-west of Bideford. Hubba himself was killed under the walls and his followers were routed, rushing back to the ships in disarray. At one spot they rallied and fought desperately to check their pursuers and give themselves the chance to reach the ships in safety.

The slaughter on both sides was so great that the place is still known as Bloody Corner. Hubba's valiant companion, Bjorn Iron-side, was among the many killed in the retreat and the worst indignity of all was when the men of Appledore captured the Danes' magical raven banner. This was a great stuffed bird which hung quiet when defeat was imminent but clapped its wings when it scented victory. Presumably its allegiance switched to whoever had possession of it. If so it must have been kept busy after its capture for only the tattered remnants of the Danish raiders staggered back alive. They buried Hubba's body beneath a cairn on the shore and this is still visible as the Hubblestone or Wibblestone.

As at Slaughterbridge in Cornwall, it is often the place-names that keep alive the memory of 'battles long ago', even when precise details of the battle itself and the protagonists have been lost or have passed over from history into legend. If, as many believe, great dramas or bloody events can leave a ripple on the ether and surface again in the same place, centuries later, Appledore should be full of ghosts. The sites of many Civil War battles, for example, are haunted by the ghosts of Cavaliers so why not the locations of earlier conflict?

Certainly many people have claimed to have heard strange shouts and sounds of battle on clear nights in North Devon. Some even say they have seen the shades of fighting men hacking one another to death or fleeing among the trees. I wish I could claim as much myself, for all apparitions have so far eluded me. Anyway the next best thing is to steep yourself in the lore and legends and keeping an open mind, visit a known site, say, round about dusk.

THE DE TRACEYS OF ILFRACOMBE

One historical figure who may still haunt Ilfracombe is Sir Will de Tracey, Baron of Barnstaple, and one of the four murderers of Thomas à Beckett. The church at Mortehoe is said to contain his tomb, although there is some doubt about this, since the brass thought to represent him bears a chalice in its right hand, the sign of

Mortehoe Church is said to contain the tomb of Sir Will de Tracey, one of the murderers of Thomas à Beckett. ▶

a priest. Still, in view of his wild deeds, the engraving could be just wishful thinking — an attempt to ingratiate himself with the Almighty. He certainly failed to do this during his life and never prospered after the crime. According to a local rhyme he even passed the curse of heaven on to his descendants for:

> *All the de Traceys*
> *Have the wind in their faces.*

It is said he hid out on Crookham Common between Mortehoe and Ilfracombe fed only by scraps from his daughter. After his death he was condemned to haunt the shore for ever, making the sand into wisps and bundles and lamenting as the storms undo his labours.

The Morte stone off Ilfracombe is likewise said to be under a curse and has been a danger to shipping for centuries. Five vessels were wrecked on it in the winter of 1852 and a piece of misogynist propaganda states that 'no power on earth can remove it except a number of wives who have dominion over their husbands' for 'a woman's hair can draw more than a yoke of oxen'.

The Morte Stone: '. . . no power on earth can remove it.'

St Helena's Church, Lundy

LUNDY ISLAND

The Morte stone is of course ascribed to the Devil as is another trap for mariners, the ridge of rocks which runs out from Clovelly and Bucks Mills towards Lundy Island. This is said to be the beginning of a causeway which Satan began to build to Lundy, but he abandoned the project when the handle of his shovel broke.

In spite of this, Lundy didn't escape unscathed as the Devil's lime-kiln testifies. This is a great fissure nearly 400 feet deep and 250 feet wide blasted out by the Old One who simply dumped the surplus rock offshore where it's now called the Shutter Rock, yet another hazard for unwary sailors.

In later years, the islanders fell victim to an unscrupulous trick prepared by the French who, during the wars in the reign of William and Mary, were considered Devils in human form. A French warship

under Dutch colours anchored in the roadstead and sent ashore for milk, pretending their captain was sick. The public-spirited islanders, convinced they were helping their allies, complied and when a few days later the 'Dutchmen' said the sick man had died, they at once gave them permission to bury him in consecrated ground and even helped carry his coffin to the church. Although it seemed rather heavy, they never suspected the nature of its contents and bowed to the foreigners' request that all the locals should leave the church during the ceremony, in line, they said, with Dutch custom.

The islanders weren't left long in suspense for the treacherous French snatched up guns and pistols hidden in the coffin, flung open the doors and proceeded to devastate the island. They herded the locals together, threatening any who tried to resist and taking their clothes to prevent them escaping. All the horses and bullocks were hamstrung and before the plunderers left, they ate and salted as many sheep and goats as they could, then tossed the rest over the cliff. After this sort of treatment it was not surprising that the islanders suffered a double dose of insularity, because of their betrayal as well as their isolated position. It was certainly many years before foreigners of whatever complexion were offered the traditional warm Lundy welcome.

THE HANGING STONE

Back on the mainland, a great stone forms the boundary mark of Combe Martin Parish. It is known as the Hanging stone, as is a similar formation on North Dartmoor and in each case the same tale is told to explain the name.

A thief stole a sheep and tied it round his neck as the easiest way to carry it home. On the way back, he rested on a rock to try to get his breath back. Sadly for him, the reverse happened, for the sheep struggled and slid over the side, strangling him. The story is not restricted to this part of Devon for there are two other formations, each known as the Hangman's Stone, one in Sidmouth and one in Leices-

◀ A glimpse of the Devil's Causeway. Satan abandoned the project to reach Lundy when his shovel broke.

tershire — and each carries a similar legend to the one at Combe Martin.

The fact that the legend is the same in each case points not so much to the same event occurring; that would seem too much of a coincidence, but to a common derivation of the names, the Saxon *stanes hengen* — hanging or uplifted stones. The legend is obviously intended to point out to any would-be thieves that crime doesn't pay, and it was probably put about by Christian moralists far more interested in ethics than etymology.

LYNTON'S VALLEY OF ROCKS

A few miles east of Combe Martin stands the spectacular Valley of Rocks near Lynton where the slate is contorted into such strange formations that, at dusk, you could swear that the valley was populated with men. One legend of the place corresponds to stories about many rock formations and standing stones — that they were once humans who were turned to stone for unseemly activities such as hurling or dancing on the Sabbath.

The Valley of Rocks is so wild and jagged that the humans are said to have been beggars led by a character called Ragged Dick who encouraged his friends to keep themselves warm with a rustic dance. As the motley crew started leaping and hopping around, a great flash of lightning split the sky and next second each was petrified as tattered columns of slate.

Years later, a castle was built on the rocks looking out to sea, a rugged fortress belonging to the Earl Sigvald who died and left it to his daughter Lady Edith. She was a headstrong and beautiful girl who was betrothed to her cousin. Like all her family she was a heathen and confided in a strange black monk who led her in her devotions to her alien gods. When her cousin, like many of the Norsemen who settled in England, accepted Christianity, she was furious and declared she would never be baptised as the gods of her forefathers were good enough for her.

◀ **The Hanging Stone: the legend points out that crime doesn't pay.**

The young earl was convinced she'd change her mind and sent a message to say he would come and claim her as his bride when next a new moon shone in the heavens. Lady Edith resolved to keep him out of the fortress and when the Black Monk offered to help her, she accepted.

'I will save the castle if you promise to be mine henceforth,' he said, 'and we'll live in it, master and mistress of Lynton for ever.' That suited her well enough and although she suspected that she was entering into a pact with the Devil, she tossed her head and didn't care. As the monk had promised, they repelled the young Earl and kept the castle for themselves, but it brought Lady Edith little joy. She became an evil-tempered harridan who sulked incessantly. One day the Monk went for a walk along the cliff-top leaving her alone. While he was gone, a Friar arrived at the castle gate.

'I bring you peace, my lady,' he said softly, 'it is the gospel of love that I preach.'

'I want no gospels here,' she screeched, 'and while I'm alive there'll be no peace in this house.' The Monk returned from his walk, leering horribly and Lady Edith turned on him in a rage.

'Throw this beggar Friar into the sea. We don't want his kind round here.' The Friar knew at once the identity of the Black Monk and made the sign of a cross. At once the Monk was stripped of his disguise and stood revealed in horns and hooves as the Devil incarnate. He grasped Lady Edith and despite her screams, flew away with her across the valley. The sky clouded over with dark lowering clouds and the cliffs beneath them heaved and swallowed the castle and all the black engines of evil it contained. The Friar knelt down and murmured a prayer of thanksgiving then looking up caught sight of the two dark and struggling figures, little more than dots blown along before a scudding wind.

Today, Lady Edith's memory is preserved in a formation known as the White Lady in the Valley of Rocks, the serenity of the stones in stark contrast to the real lady's horrifying end.

'He grasped Lady Edith and, despite her ▶
screams, flew away with her across the valley.'

THE DOONES OF BADGWORTHY

For some reason North Devon and Exmoor seem to attract the blackest villains of all, villains like the infamous Doone family who really existed outside the pages of *Lorna Doone*. Although they lived over the border in Somerset, I'm claiming them as legends of Devon because they committed so many of their fabled atrocities during raids to the west.

It is said that the family were originally Scottish free-booters who moved south to Badgworthy near Simonsbath at the time of Cromwell and proceeded to terrorise the neighbourhood, blackmailing farmers and murdering as the mood took them. Some remains of

Left: Lynton's Valley of Rocks. Below: Exmoor.
'. . . North Devon and Exmoor seem to attract the blackest villains . . .'

buildings survive a mile from Mole's Chamber in a bottom called the Warren and it is here they may have lived, like the Gubbings 'in cotts, rather holes than houses, like swine'. From all accounts 'their wealth consisted of other men's goods', but they are chiefly remembered for their brutality and the real delight they took in an almost comically exaggerated heartlessness.

In one tale, which I hope was legend rather than truth, they broke into a house, bent on robbery and murdered an infant, instructing the child, 'If anyone asks who killed thee, Tell 'em 'twas the Doones of Badgery.' On another raid, the woman of the house hid in an oven to escape from them, but the Doones, suspecting she was in the house, slit her young daughter's throat, chuckling, 'kill the calf and the cow will howl.' The mother of course could not bear to watch her child slaughtered and burst out of the oven, only to suffer a similar fate.

It was after these outrages that the local people rioted and a party of peasantry armed with billhooks and blunderbusses marched on the Doone's stronghold, capturing the entire clan in a pitched battle. The few that escaped the summary rough justice the peasants meted out were tried for their crimes and, as in all the best stories of retribution, hanged, drawn and quartered.

BAMPFYLDE-MOORE CAREW

In complete contrast to the Doones was Bampfylde Carew, a confidence trickster and self-styled lovable rogue who dictated a highly sensationalised version of his autobiography to a literary acquaintance. He was born in 1693, son of Reverend Theodore Carew, the rector of Bickleigh near Tiverton and at the age of twelve he was sent to Tiverton School. He did not have a distinguished school career. He and some other boys kept a pack of hounds and during a hunt, these chased a deer over standing corn, causing so much damage that the farmer complained to the headmaster. Bampfylde was too great a coward to take his whipping and ran away from school to join

◀ **'The Doones, terrorised the neighbourhood, blackmailing farmers and murdering as the mood took them.'**

Exmoor — the haunt of the Doones.

a group of gipsies. He grew to love the applause he won for his low
cunning and soon nothing would induce him to return to civilisation.
In spite of this, he dictated this description of himself and only mod-
esty is absent from the list of virtues he claims. It is a description
which bears strong resemblances to Fielding's *Tom Jones*, another
rogue with whom Carew identified strongly:

'The Stature of our Hero is tall and majestic, his limbs strong and
well-proportioned, his Features regular, his Countenance open and
ingenuous, bearing all those characteristical Marks which Physio-
gnomists assert denote an honest and good-natured Mind.' If this
was true, Carew's appearance belied his character for he was adept
at all types of disguise. Sometimes he posed as a shipwrecked sailor
and took advantage of people's generosity; sometimes he claimed his

house had burnt down; sometimes he capered around in a blanket pretending to be an escaped lunatic. He also kept a watchful eye on the papers for disasters and as soon as he heard of one he would claim to have lost everything in it and apply for relief. He backed up his story with forged letters, supposedly from magistrates and clergymen. He certainly worked at his 'trade', making a voyage to Newfoundland simply to pass himself off more convincingly as a shipwrecked sailor with detailed knowledge of the places, merchants, and agents there. This dedication paid off, for although he'd made a lot of money before, it was nothing compared to what he could now command.

Perhaps his worst act of all was when he sailed from Dartmouth to Newcastle in a coal ship and fell in love with a doctor's daughter, Miss Gray, passing himself off as the ship's mate and gaining her affections. Her father objected to the match so Carew induced her to elope with him to Dartmouth. It was only there that he confessed the only trade he knew was that of a rat-catcher. By the standards of that time, she had taken an irrevocable step in running away with him, so she consented to go through with the marriage in Bath. The two lived in high style there for a few weeks until his money was gone and he was forced to return to his fraudulent ways, inadvertently helped by his uncle, a clergyman who took the young couple in, determined to reform his nephew.

Carew spent the time studying his uncle's manner and speech and when he left his house, took with him cassock gown and bands, then went on to make more money than ever, impersonating a clergyman who had fallen on hard times.

His cunning and utter unscrupulousness gained him such credit among the gipsies and tramps of England that when their leader, Claude Patch, died, Carew was elected King of the Beggars in his stead at a great gathering in London. Eventually he was arrested, tried at Exeter quarter-sessions and transported to Maryland. He was sold to a planter but escaped almost immediately, still bearing the iron collar of slavery. He met a group of Indians and persuaded them to relieve him of his collar, then true to form, stole a canoe from his benefactors and imposed on several families before embarking for Bristol at New London.

Carew was frightened that he would be pressed for the Navy as he approached England, so he pricked his chest and arms with a needle and rubbed gun-powder and bay salt into the wounds to simulate

smallpox. When an officer boarded the ship to see if there were any likely men aboard, he was at once put ashore for fear of infection.

He continued to beg for his living and met up with a like-minded companion who shared his life of crime for several weeks. Unknown to Carew, the companion was none other than Viscount Weymouth, who also enjoyed impersonating beggars, and he decided to give the imposter a taste of his own medicine. Leaving Carew in an ale-house, he slipped home and resumed his normal clothes, then ordered his servants to go out and find a certain mendicant sailor.

When Carew was brought before him, Lord Weymouth accused him fiercely of thieving and imposture and threatened him with prison. By this time Carew was sweating with fear and Lord Weymouth left him to stew before returning dressed again in rags, pretending that he too had been caught. The two compared stories so that their accounts should tally and Carew was examined a second time, by Lord Weymouth's steward. While this was going on, Weymouth changed back into his finery and Carew was ushered into his presence to receive sentence. By this time, the prisoner was expecting transportation or a long prison term at the very least, but Lord Weymouth burst out laughing, revealed his dual identity and took him off for a day at Warminster races.

Despite a life entirely given to inventive rascality, Carew came off surprisingly well, though with his talent for high comedy, his leadership and his boldness, he would probably have succeeded at whatever he turned his hand to. Up to his death in 1758 he displayed great imagination, and even pretended to be a soldier wounded at Fontenoy, exhibiting a raw beefsteak strapped to his knee as his open wound. According to his autobiography his disguises were endless, but if they had all been true he would have needed several lifetimes to put them into practice. As it was, some at least were invented or exaggerated à la Baron Munchausen, but he recounted them with such verve and vigour that if he had not chosen a life of begging and imposture, he could have made a fortune as a writer of highly-coloured fiction.

◄ Bampfylde-Moore Carew, 'confidence trickster and self-styled lovable rogue.'

MATTHEW THE MILLER

One man who would have deeply disapproved of the doings of Bampfylde Carew was a miller named Matthew, who lived in Exeter centuries ago. He worked in Cricklepit Lane with his two sons and was an upright and punctual soul, so punctual that the people of Exeter swore they could set their clocks by him.

''Tis no good,' he declared, 'when volks is waitin' to bake their bread to be still-a-grindin' the corn. Rise with the sun and take note of the passing of the hours till 'er do set again and naught shall be spoiled on account of waitin' for 'ee.' One day old Matthew died and the Exeter folk were inconsolable at the loss of his cheerful face, but they had another reason to mourn his passing.

'Matthew the Miller is dead. He was our clock, so what shall we do now?' they asked sadly, and for three months everything was at sixes and sevens. Then a rare clock was installed in the tower of the church of St Mary's steps in the Westgate. Everyone gathered round to see it and to their delight the figure of Matthew the Miller nodded the hour as the clock struck. His sons stood on either side of him and they came out to strike the quarters, hammering two great bells.

Although some learned people claimed that the figures really represented King Henry VIII and two men-at-arms, the people of Exeter knew that it was no-one so royal and remote and the children made up a rhyme to commemorate their beloved miller:

Matthew the miller's alive, Matthew the miller is dead
For every hour in Westgate tower, Old Matthew nods his head.

The clock still exists in the ancient Westgate and until recently, one man had to climb the steep steps of the tower to wind it. He has now been supplanted by an automatic winding mechanism, but in spite of this, Matthew and his sons are still as timely as ever.

THE PARSON AND HIS CLERK

Exemplary characters like Matthew are very much the exception in the legends for folklore seems to thrive on baddies — and the blacker

'Matthew the Miller' Clock in Westgate, Exeter.

91

the better. One such evil man was a priest who wanted above everything to become Bishop of Exeter and was promised the See when it next became vacant. He was filled with a most unchristian delight when he learnt that the present Bishop was ill and he was heard to murmur 'Nothing trivial I trust' as he pressed the messenger for more details.

The invalid was sent to Dawlish and the priest began visiting him with a ghoulish frequency, accompanied by his clerk. The two were crossing Haldon Hill one day on their weekly visit when a storm blew up and they lost their way.

The priest flew into a towering rage; 'You stupid fool, I'd rather have the Devil himself as a guide.' As any student of folklore will know, these are about the most foolish words, anyone, particularly a cleric can utter, for at once a dark stranger seemed to materialise out of the nearest bog.

'I see you two gentlemen are lost,' he said in a peculiar wheedling tone. 'Allow me to guide you to Dawlish, for I too live there and I would be delighted if you would accept my hospitality.'

'Very civil of you, my dear fellow,' responded the priest, fully restored to good-humour and the three set off and soon arrived at a brightly-lit mansion, throbbing with sounds of revelry.

'My humble abode,' said the stranger. 'Won't you stay for dinner before you go on your way?' Tired and hungry, the two agreed and sat down to a sumptuous meal in the midst of a party. Only one thing puzzled the priest; among the revellers he kept seeing the faces of colleagues he'd always supposed were dead, but the wine was good and the brandy better so he soon paid no attention and scolded the clerk when he remarked on the same phenomenon. Just as they finished, a messenger arrived at the door bringing news of the Bishop's death. The priest was overjoyed and thanking his host warmly, made ready to leave. As they picked their way down the long drive, the priest glanced back and saw the mansion transformed into a pile of jagged rocks, the guests to shrieking spectres and the music replaced by a hideous howling like souls in torment. Terrified for his life, the priest glanced down and already the swirling incoming tide was lapping at his horse's belly.

The bodies of the two horses were found on the shore the next day,

◀ 'The guests were transformed to shrieking spectres.'

but neither parson nor clerk was ever seen again, although two mysterious rocks appeared from nowhere overnight. The rocks, one bigger than the other, still make a spectacular landmark a mile and a half east of Teignmouth and because of their contrasting size and the circumstances of their arrival, they could only be known as the Parson and the Clerk.

DADDYHOLE LEAP

The parson should have known just how foolish it was to call on the name of the Devil in vain, but other victims encounter him by chance in one of his many disguises, and enter into a pact quite unwittingly.

A young Torquay girl fell in love with a local boy but he jilted her on their wedding day. She went almost mad with grief and jealousy and wandered up and down the shore, plotting revenge which she never had the courage to carry out. One night she was bowled over by the Wild Hunt and catching sight of the Devil on his huge horse, furiously whipping his Wish hounds, she fainted dead away.

When she came to, the beach was deserted and she was being revived by a handsome young man. He was so sympathetic that she confided all her troubles to him. They met more and more often and he promised to help her get her revenge if she would vow to be his. She agreed and he gave her a long, curiously carved knife, saying that her erstwhile lover would meet his new love at Daddy's Hole, at the top of the cliff overlooking the cove.

She lay in wait for them and just as the two embraced, she rushed out and stabbed them both through the heart. Next moment she heard a noise like a great storm and the beating of many wings. The whole sky darkened as the Wild Hunt swept down on her and she gasped in horror, for at their head sat her handsome young man on a headless steed. He was the Demon Huntsman himself, come to hold her to her rash promise. He reined in his horse, swept up the girl under one arm then leapt over the cliff into the depths of Daddy's Hole and was never seen again.

◄ The Parson and the Clerk: 'two mysterious
rocks appeared from nowhere overnight.'

TOM CROCKER OF BURGH ISLAND

Round the coast from Torquay, Burgh Island in Bigbury Bay boasts a spectacular hotel which in the thirties was one of the most celebrated in Europe and attracted every jet-setter of the time, including Mary Pickford, Douglas Fairbanks, King Farouk and Noel Coward. Before that, the island's most famous resident was a pirate named Tom Crocker who made it his hide-out until he was caught and hanged in 1395 and it's said that he still walks the island every year in the third week in August, the anniversary of his execution.

Up to a few years ago the bright young things at the hotel organised celebrations on that date and everyone went out looking for him, perhaps a rash move if he was as evil as he's painted. Despite their efforts though, he was never found and the whole affair sounds like a good excuse for a party rather than a serious ghost-hunt. All the same, his spirit could still be hanging around for the hotel's present owner, Susan Waugh, confesses that she experiences an almost tangible feeling of melancholy around the gateway where the hanging took place, while many dogs refuse to pass the spot.

My favourite relic of Tom Crocker is the face said to be his etched in the granite chimney-breast of the wonderful little pub at the bottom of the hotel drive. Although it is a natural formation, I could see nose and eye sockets distinctly and when I put a lighted cigarette between his pursed lips, Tom performed his party piece and smoked it down to the filter. Pub bores will scoff and say that it's only the draught from the fire, but I prefer to imagine Tom Crocker who died long before tobacco arrived in this country learning a modern vice and chuckling as he enjoys a quiet drag on his cigarette.

THE GREAT DEVON MYSTERY

As someone who would very much like to believe in the Supernatural, despite positive proof either way, the people I most resent

◀ 'He was the Demon Huntsman himself . . .'

are the rationalists who try to find the most mundane explanations for any phenomenon however wondrous and then bludgeon the imaginative or simply undecided into submission with their own pedestrian fancies; for 'Philosophy will clip an angel's wings'.

Just as, in our imperfect state of knowledge, the greatest religions still require a leap of Faith and cannot be explained in rational terms, some of the strongest legends are based on mystery and on quirky, inexplicable elements which defy reason and turn our everyday assumptions upside down. One such assumption is the scientist's war-cry, 'There's a reason for everything', and I take an anarchic delight in the sort of happening which will fit into no cosy pigeonhole and remains outside the comprehension of any single blanket theory.

In a world full of Surrey pumas and Bermuda triangles, Devon can still boast one of the longest-running mysteries of all time, still unsolved after 125 years. A letter to *The Times* in February 1855 summarises what happened:

'It appears that on Thursday night last, there was a very heavy fall of snow in the neighbourhood of Exeter and the south of Devon. On the following morning, the inhabitants of the above towns were surprised at discovering the tracks of some strange and mysterious animal, endowed with the power of ubiquity as the footprints were to be seen in all kinds of inaccessible places — on the tops of houses and narrow walls, in gardens and courtyards enclosed by high walls and palings as well as in open fields. There was hardly a garden in Lympstone where the footprints were not observed.

'The track appeared more like that of a biped than a quadruped and the steps were generally eight inches in advance of each other. The impressions of the feet closely resembled that of a donkey's shoe.'

In the course of a lively correspondence in *The Times* and the *Illustrated London News*, further details came to light. The 'Devil's footprints' were found to stretch for a distance of over 100 miles. At one point they jumped over the two-mile wide Exe estuary and continued, seemingly unperturbed by the gigantic leap, still an even eight and a half inches apart. They were found on either side of a haystack which was untouched and on either side of a fourteen foot

◀ Tom Crocker: 'I put a lighted cigarette between his lips.'

wall. At one point they even came to the top of a drainpipe and re-appeared at the bottom, like the wooden rat in my favourite fête game of 'Bash the rat'. A strange feature of the prints was that they were placed one in front of another unlike a normal animal trail.

As this was the high peak of Victorian rationalism, a fine crop of theories soon evolved to try to explain away the mystery. They in-cluded otters, leaping rats, and a rope trailing from a balloon. Pro-fessor Owen, the man who discovered that the Daedalus sea-serpent was really a seal, stated authoritatively that the prints were caused by badgers.

All the explanations were convincing but none of them accounted for everything, none, that is except for the local theory that the marks were indeed the Devil's footprints. Of course this explanation is anathema to scientists and pub bores alike, but 'there are more things in heaven and earth' . . . and the Devil already has an impres-sive track record of appearances throughout the county. So while the earnest seekers after truth fail to provide me with a theory that is either intellectually or imaginatively satisfying, I shall continue to believe that on that snowy February night in South Devon and at countless other times and other places, from Lundy Island to Daddy-hole Cove

'just as plain to see, the devil walks'.

◀ ' . . . just as plain to see the devil walks'.

BIBLIOGRAPHY

Crossing's Guide to Dartmoor
The Folklore of Devon, Ralph Whitlock.
Popular Romances of the West of England, Robert Hunt.
By-gone days in Devon and Cornwall, Whitcombe.
Folk Tales of Devon, V. Day Sharman.
Trojans in the West Country, Theo Brown, Toucan Press.
Dartmoor Legends, Eva Rogers, Pilgrim Press.
Phenomena, John Michell and Robert J.M. Rickard, Thames and Hudson.
Historia Regum Britanniae, Geoffrey of Monmouth.
Survey of Cornwall, Carew.
Tales and Legends, Jennifer Westwood, Hart-Davis.
The Devil in Devon, J.R.W. Coxhead.
A Sampler of British Folk-Tales, Katharine M. Briggs, Routledge and Kegan Paul.
A true relation of the apparition 1641, J. Oxenham.
Devonshire Studies, W.G. Hoskins and H.P.R. Finberg, Jonathan Cape, Bodley Head.
Devonshire Characters and Strange Events, S. Baring-Gould.
Legends of Exmoor, Jack Hurley.
Devon Traditions and Fairy tales, J.R.W. Coxhead.
A description of the parts of Devonshire bordering the Tamar and the Tavy, Mrs Bray, 1836.
A Book of Folk-lore, S. Baring-Gould.
Haunted England, C.R. Hole.
English Folk-Lore, C.R. Hole.
Folk-tales of England, Ruth L. Tongue.
A Survey of Devon, Risdon.
Worthies of England, Fuller.

ALSO AVAILABLE

LEGENDS OF CORNWALL
by Sally Jones. 60 photographs and drawings. Price
Brilliantly illustrated with many photographs and vivid drawings of legendary characters. The Author, who is a member of Westward Television, makes a journey through the legendary sites of Cornwall, beginning at the Tamar and ending at Land's End.
'Highly readable and beautifully romantic . . .' Desmond Lyons, Cornwall Courier.

THE PLYMOUTH BLITZ
by Frank Wintle. 66 photographs. Price
This is the story of the horrific events that put Plymouth in the front line of the war, and the controversial rebuilding — and rebirth of the City.
'Frank Wintle has written a thought-provoking book . . . he and Bossiney are to be congratulated for their service to the City.' George Harris, Midweek Independent

DEVON MYSTERIES
by Judy Chard. 22 photographs.
Devon is not only a beautiful county, it's a mysterious place too — and if anybody had any doubts about that, Judy Chard demolishes them with her exploration into the strange and often the inexplicable. This book, though, is not just about *mysterious Devon*, it's essentially about *Devon mysteries*.
'. . . my appetite for unexplained happenings has been truly whetted by Newton Abbot author Judy Chard's latest offering.' Mid Devon Advertiser

OCCULT IN THE WEST
by Michael Williams. Over 30 photographs.
Michael Williams follows his successful *Supernatural in Cornwall* with further interviews and investigations into the Occult — this time incorporating Devon. Ghosts and clairvoyancy, dreams and psychic painting, healing and hypnosis are only some of the facets of a fascinating story.
'. . . provides the doubters with much food for thought.'
Jean Kenzie, Tavistock Gazette

MY DARTMOOR
by Clive Gunnell of Westward TV — television's most famous walker.
Map and 12 pages of photographs and drawings of Dartmoor wildlife by Robin Armstrong.
'The work is that of a merry man, and an observant, though kindly one.'
Western Morning News

THE SOUTH HAMS

by Judy Chard. 55 photographs and map.

Salcombe, Kingsbridge, Hope Cove and Hallsands are only some of the places that make up the patchwork of the South Hams. Judy Chard tells of fishing villages destroyed by the sea, of shipwrecks and of the evacuation of the South Hams for D Day.

'Solid history, lively stories and fine photos make this an attractive and rewarding study.'
The Woman Journalist

DARTMOOR PRISON

by Rufus Endle. 35 photographs.

A vivid portrait of the famous prison on the moor stretching from 1808 — with rare photographs taken inside today.

'The bleak Devon cage's 170 year history . . . fascinatingly sketched by one of the Westcountry's best known journalists Rufus Endle . . . the man with the key to Dartmoor.'
Western Daily Press

ABOUT WIDECOMBE

43 photographs.

A personal portrait of the beautiful Devonshire village. Interviews with characters like Uncle Tom Cobley and the Widecombe Wag, researches into Widecombe's colourful past, including its world-famous Fair and Song.

'A warmly recommended read for all who love Devon — and Dartmoor in particular.'
The Independent.

ALONG THE DART

by Judy Chard. 34 photographs and 2 maps.

Judy Chard takes us on a journey up the River Dart from historic Dartmouth and the sea to its beginning on Dartmoor. It is a journey lovingly told. Past and present, people and animals, boats and buildings, she recaptures them all.

'. . . full of facts, anecdotes, and legends about the river and its surrounding area and people . . .'
Roy Derwent, Express & Echo

LUNDY ISLAND

by Joan Rendell. 40 photographs and map.

Joan Rendell explores Lundy Past and Lundy Present, proving in the process that it was — and remains — a world of its own.

'Magical and alluring . . .'
Irene Roberts, The South Hams Newspapers

ALONG THE LEMON

35 photographs.

Judy Chard puts one of Devon's lesser-known rivers on the map. The revised edition also features the 1979 Newton Abbot floods.

'. . . in prose and pictures, the story of the river from its rising near Haytor, its junction with the Sig and final pouring into the Teign.'
Herald Express